# The Sacred Wood
## and
## Major Early Essays

## T. S. ELIOT

DOVER PUBLICATIONS, INC.
Mineola, New York

*Bibliographical Note*

The Sacred Wood and Major Early Essays, first published by Dover in 1998, is a republication of The Sacred Wood. published by Methuen & Co., Ltd., London, 1920, along with the following essays first published in The Times Literary Supplement: "Andrew Marvell," (March 31, 1921); "John Dryden," (June 9, 1921); and "The Metaphysical Poets," (October 20, 1921).

*Library of Congress Cataloging-in-Publication Data*

Eliot, T. S. (Thomas Stearns), 1888–1965.
    The sacred wood and major early essays / T. S. Eliot.
        p.    cm.
    ISBN-13: 978-0-486-29936-5
    ISBN-10: 0-486-29936-8
    1. Criticism.    2. Literature.    I. Title.
PN511.E44    1998
809—dc21                                                                98-7702
                                                                          CIP

Manufactured in the United States by LSC Communications
29936806        2018
www.doverpublications.com

# Contents

# Introduction

To anyone who is at all capable of experiencing the pleasures of justice, it is gratifying to be able to make amends to a writer whom one has vaguely depreciated for some years. The faults and foibles of Matthew Arnold are no less evident to me now than twelve years ago, after my first admiration for him; but I hope that now, on re-reading some of his prose with more care, I can better appreciate his position. And what makes Arnold seem all the more remarkable is, that if he were our exact contemporary, he would find all his labour to perform again. A moderate number of persons have engaged in what is called "critical" writing, but no conclusion is any more solidly established than it was in 1865. In the first essay in the first *Essays in Criticism* we read that

> it has long seemed to me that the burst of creative activity in our literature, through the first quarter of this century, had about it in fact something premature; and that from this cause its productions are doomed, most of them, in spite of the sanguine hopes which accompanied and do still accompany them, to prove hardly more lasting than the productions of far less splendid epochs. And this prematureness comes from its having proceeded without having its proper data, without sufficient material to work with. In other words, the English poetry of the first quarter of this century, with plenty of energy, plenty of creative force, did not know enough. This makes Byron so empty of matter, Shelley so incoherent, Wordsworth even, profound as he is, yet so wanting in completeness and variety.

This judgment of the Romantic Generation has not, so far as I know, ever been successfully controverted; and it has not, so far as I know, ever made very much impression on popular opinion. Once a poet is accepted, his reputation is seldom disturbed, for better or worse. So little impression has Arnold's opinion made, that his statement will probably be as true of the first quarter of the twentieth century as it was of the nineteenth. A few sentences later, Arnold articulates the nature of the malady:

iv

In the Greece of Pindar and Sophocles, in the England of Shakespeare, the poet lived in a current of ideas in the highest degree animating and nourishing to the creative power; society was, in the fullest measure, permeated by fresh thought, intelligent and alive; and this state of things is the true basis for the creative power's exercise, in this it finds its data, its materials, truly ready for its hand; all the books and reading in the world are only valuable as they are helps to this.

At this point Arnold is indicating the centre of interest and activity of the critical intelligence; and it is at this perception, we may almost say, that Arnold's critical activity stopped. In a society in which the arts were seriously studied, in which the art of writing was respected, Arnold might have become a critic. How astonishing it would be, if a man like Arnold had concerned himself with the art of the novel, had compared Thackeray with Flaubert, had analysed the work of Dickens, had shown his contemporaries exactly why the author of *Amos Barton* is a more *serious* writer than Dickens, and why the author of *La Chartreuse de Parme* is more serious than either? In *Culture and Anarchy*, in *Literature and Dogma*, Arnold was not occupied so much in establishing a criticism as in attacking the uncritical. The difference is that while in constructive work something can be done, destructive work must incessantly be repeated; and furthermore Arnold, in his destruction, went for game outside of the literary preserve altogether, much of it political game untouched and inviolable by ideas. This activity of Arnold's we must regret; it might perhaps have been carried on as effectively, if not quite so neatly, by some disciple (had there been one) in an editorial position on a newspaper. Arnold is not to be blamed: he wasted his strength, as men of superior ability sometimes do, because he saw something to be done and no one else to do it. The temptation, to any man who is interested in ideas and primarily in literature, to put literature into the corner until he has cleaned up the whole country first, is almost irresistible. Some persons, like Mr. Wells and Mr. Chesterton, have succeeded so well in this latter profession of setting the house in order, and have attracted so much more attention than Arnold, that we must conclude that it is indeed their proper rôle, and that they have done well for themselves in laying literature aside.

Not only is the critic tempted outside of criticism. The criticism proper betrays such poverty of ideas and such atrophy of sensibility that men who ought to preserve their critical ability for the improvement of their own creative work are tempted into criticism. I do not intend from this the usually silly inference that the "creative" gift is "higher" than the crit-

ical. When one creative mind is better than another, the reason often is
that the better is the more critical. But the great bulk of the work of criticism could be done by minds of the second order, and it is just these
minds of the second order that are difficult to find. They are necessary
for the rapid circulation of ideas. The periodical press—the ideal literary
periodical—is an instrument of transport; and the literary periodical
press is dependent upon the existence of a sufficient number of second-
order (I do not say "second-rate," the word is too derogatory) minds to
supply its material. These minds are necessary for that "current of ideas,"
that "society permeated by fresh thought," of which Arnold speaks.

It is a perpetual heresy of English culture to believe that only the first-
order mind, the Genius, the Great Man, matters; that he is solitary, and
produced best in the least favourable environment, perhaps the Public
School; and that it is most likely a sign of inferiority that Paris can show
so many minds of the second order. If too much bad verse is published in
London, it does not occur to us to raise our standards, to do anything to
educate the poetasters; the remedy is, Kill them off. I quote from Mr.
Edmund Gosse:[1]

> Unless something is done to stem this flood of poetastry the art of
> verse will become not merely superfluous, but ridiculous. Poetry is
> not a formula which a thousand flappers and hobbledehoys ought to
> be able to master in a week without any training, and the mere fact
> that it seems to be now practised with such universal ease is enough
> to prove that something has gone amiss with our standards. . . . This
> is all wrong, and will lead us down into the abyss like so many
> Gadarene swine unless we resist it.

We quite agree that poetry is not a formula. But what does Mr. Gosse
propose to do about it? If Mr. Gosse had found himself in the flood of
poetastry in the reign of Elizabeth, what would he have done about it?
would he have stemmed it? What exactly is this abyss? and if something
"has gone amiss with our standards," is it wholly the fault of the younger
generation that it is aware of no authority that it must respect? It is part
of the business of the critic to preserve tradition—where a good tradition
exists. It is part of his business to see literature steadily and to see it
whole; and this is eminently to see it *not* as consecrated by time, but to see
it beyond time; to see the best work of our time and the best work of

---

[1] *Sunday Times,* May 30, 1920.

twenty-five hundred years ago with the same eyes.[2] It is part of his business to help the poetaster to understand his own limitations. The poetaster who understands his own limitations will be one of our useful second-order minds; a good minor poet (something which is very rare) or another good critic. As for the first-order minds, when they happen, they will be none the worse off for a "current of ideas"; the solitude with which they will always and everywhere be invested is a very different thing from isolation, or a monarchy of death.

NOTE.—I may commend as a model to critics who desire to correct some of the poetical vagaries of the present age, the following passage from a writer who cannot be accused of flaccid leniency, and the justice of whose criticism must be acknowledged even by those who feel a strong partiality toward the school of poets criticized:—

> Yet great labour, directed by great abilities, is never wholly lost; if they frequently threw away their wit upon false conceits, they likewise sometimes struck out unexpected truth: if their conceits were far-fetched, they were often worth the carriage. To write on their plan, it was at least necessary to read and think. No man could be born a metaphysical poet, nor assume the dignity of a writer, by descriptions copied from descriptions, by imitations borrowed from imitations, by traditional imagery, and hereditary similes, by readiness of rhyme, and volubility of syllables.
>
> In perusing the works of this race of authors, the mind is exercised either by recollection or inquiry: something already learned is to be retrieved, or something new is to be examined. If their greatness seldom elevates, their acuteness often surprises; if the imagination is not always gratified, at least the powers of reflection and comparison are employed; and in the mass of materials which ingenious absurdity has thrown together, genuine wit and useful knowledge may be sometimes found buried perhaps in grossness of expression, but useful to those who know their value; and such as, when they are expanded to perspicuity, and polished to elegance, may give lustre to works which have more propriety though less copiousness of sentiment.—JOHNSON, *Life of Cowley.*

---

[2] Arnold, it must be admitted, gives us often the impression of seeing the masters, whom he quotes, as canonical literature, rather than as masters.

For
H. W. E.
"Tacuit et Fecit"

"INTRAVIT pinacothecam senex canus, exercitati vultus et qui videretur nescio quid magnum promittere, sed cultu non proinde speciosus, et facile appareret eum ex hac nota litteratum esse, quos odisse divites solent . . . 'ego' inquit 'poeta sum et ut spero, non humillimi spiritus, si modo coronis aliquid credendum est, quas etiam ad immeritos deferre gratia solet.'"—PETRONIUS.

"I also like to dine on becaficas."

Certain of these essays appeared, in the same or a more primitive form, in *The Times Literary Supplement, The Athenæum, Art and Letters,* and *The Egoist.* The author desires to express his obligation to the editors of these periodicals.

# THE SACRED WOOD

## THE PERFECT CRITIC

### I

"Eriger en lois ses impressions personnelles, c'est le grand effort d'un homme s'il est sincère."—*Lettres à l'Amazone.*

COLERIDGE was perhaps the greatest of English critics, and in a sense the last. After Coleridge we have Matthew Arnold; but Arnold—I think it will be conceded—was rather a propagandist for criticism than a critic, a popularizer rather than a creator of ideas. So long as this island remains an island (and we are no nearer the Continent than were Arnold's contemporaries) the work of Arnold will be important; it is still a bridge across the Channel, and it will always have been good sense. Since Arnold's attempt to correct his countrymen, English criticism has followed two directions. When a distinguished critic observed recently, in a newspaper article, that "poetry is the most highly organized form of intellectual activity," we were conscious that we were reading neither Coleridge nor Arnold. Not only have the words "organized" and "activity," occurring together in this phrase, that familiar vague suggestion of the scientific vocabulary which is characteristic of modern writing, but one asked questions which Coleridge and Arnold would not have permitted one to ask. How is it, for instance, that poetry is more "highly organized" than astronomy, physics, or pure mathematics, which we imagine to be, in relation to the scientist who practises them, "intellectual activity" of a pretty highly organized type? "Mere strings of words," our critic continues with felicity and truth, "flung like dabs of paint across a blank canvas, may awaken surprise ... but have no significance whatever in the history of literature." The phrases by which Arnold is best known may be inadequate, they may assemble more doubts than they dispel, but they usually

1

have some meaning. And if a phrase like "the most highly organized form of intellectual activity" is the highest organization of thought of which contemporary criticism, in a distinguished representative, is capable, then, we conclude, modern criticism is degenerate.

The verbal disease above noticed may be reserved for diagnosis by and by. It is not a disease from which Mr. Arthur Symons (for the quotation was, of course, not from Mr. Symons) notably suffers. Mr. Symons represents the other tendency; he is a representative of what is always called "æsthetic criticism" or "impressionistic criticism." And it is this form of criticism which I propose to examine at once. Mr. Symons, the critical successor of Pater, and partly of Swinburne (I fancy that the phrase "sick or sorry" is the common property of all three), *is* the "impressionistic critic." He, if anyone, would be said to expose a sensitive and cultivated mind—cultivated, that is, by the accumulation of a considerable variety of impressions from all the arts and several languages—before an "object"; and his criticism, if anyone's, would be said to exhibit to us, like the plate, the faithful record of the impressions, more numerous or more refined than our own, upon a mind more sensitive than our own. A record, we observe, which is also an interpretation, a translation; for it must itself impose impressions upon us, and these impressions are as much created as transmitted by the criticism. I do not say at once that this is Mr. Symons; but it is the "impressionistic" critic, and the impressionistic critic is supposed to be Mr. Symons.

At hand is a volume which we may test.[1] Ten of these thirteen essays deal with single plays of Shakespeare, and it is therefore fair to take one of these ten as a specimen of the book:

> *Antony and Cleopatra* is the most wonderful, I think, of all Shakespeare's plays . . .

and Mr. Symons reflects that Cleopatra is the most wonderful of all women:

> The queen who ends the dynasty of the Ptolemies has been the star of poets, a malign star shedding baleful light, from Horace and Propertius down to Victor Hugo; and it is not to poets only . . .

What, we ask, is this for? as a page on Cleopatra, and on her possible origin in the dark lady of the Sonnets, unfolds itself. And we find, gradually, that

---

[1] *Studies in Elizabethan Drama.* By Arthur Symons.

this is not an essay on a work of art or a work of intellect; but that Mr. Symons is living through the play as one might live it through in the theatre; recounting, commenting:

> In her last days Cleopatra touches a certain elevation . . . she would die a thousand times, rather than live to be a mockery and a scorn in men's mouths . . . she is a woman to the last . . . so she dies . . . the play ends with a touch of grave pity . . .

Presented in this rather unfair way, torn apart like the leaves of an artichoke, the impressions of Mr. Symons come to resemble a common type of popular literary lecture, in which the stories of plays or novels are retold, the motives of the characters set forth, and the work of art therefore made easier for the beginner. But this is not Mr. Symons' reason for writing. The reason why we find a similarity between his essay and this form of education is that *Antony and Cleopatra* is a play with which we are pretty well acquainted, and of which we have, therefore, our own impressions. We can please ourselves with our own impressions of the characters and their emotions; and we do not find the impressions of another person, however sensitive, very significant. But if we can recall the time when we were ignorant of the French symbolists, and met with *The Symbolist Movement in Literature*, we remember that book as an introduction to wholly new feelings, as a revelation. After we have read Verlaine and Laforgue and Rimbaud and return to Mr. Symons' book, we may find that our own impressions dissent from his. The book has not, perhaps, a permanent value for the one reader, but it has led to results of permanent importance for him.

The question is not whether Mr. Symons' impressions are "true" or "false." So far as you can isolate the "impression," the pure feeling, it is, of course, neither true nor false. The point is that you never rest at the pure feeling; you react in one of two ways, or, as I believe Mr. Symons does, in a mixture of the two ways. The moment you try to put the impressions into words, you either begin to analyse and construct, to "ériger en lois," or you begin to create something else. It is significant that Swinburne, by whose poetry Mr. Symons may at one time have been influenced, is one man in his poetry and a different man in his criticism; to this extent and in this respect only, that he is satisfying a different impulse; he is criticizing, expounding, arranging. You may say this is not the criticism of a critic, that it is emotional, not intellectual—though of this there are two opinions, but it is in the direction of analysis and construction, a beginning to "ériger en lois," and not in the direction of creation. So I infer that

Swinburne found an adequate outlet for the creative impulse in his poetry; and none of it was forced back and out through his critical prose. The style of the latter is essentially a prose style; and Mr. Symons' prose is much more like Swinburne's poetry than it is like his prose. I imagine—though here one's thought is moving in almost complete darkness—that Mr. Symons is far more disturbed, far more profoundly affected, by his reading than was Swinburne, who responded rather by a violent and immediate and comprehensive burst of admiration which may have left him internally unchanged. The disturbance in Mr. Symons is almost, but not quite, to the point of creating; the reading sometimes fecundates his emotions to produce something new which is not criticism, but is not the expulsion, the ejection, the birth of creativeness.

The type is not uncommon, although Mr. Symons is far superior to most of the type. Some writers are essentially of the type that reacts in excess of the stimulus, making something new out of the impressions, but suffer from a defect of vitality or an obscure obstruction which prevents nature from taking its course. Their sensibility alters the object, but never transforms it. Their reaction is that of the ordinary emotional person developed to an exceptional degree. For this ordinary emotional person, experiencing a work of art, has a mixed critical and creative reaction. It is made up of comment and opinion, and also new emotions which are vaguely applied to his own life. The sentimental person, in whom a work of art arouses all sorts of emotions which have nothing to do with that work of art whatever, but are accidents of personal association, is an incomplete artist. For in an artist these suggestions made by a work of art, which are purely personal, become fused with a multitude of other suggestions from multitudinous experience, and result in the production of a new object which is no longer purely personal, because it is a work of art itself.

It would be rash to speculate, and is perhaps impossible to determine, what is unfulfilled in Mr. Symons' charming verse that overflows into his critical prose. Certainly we may say that in Swinburne's verse the circuit of impression and expression is complete; and Swinburne was therefore able, in his criticism, to be more a critic than Mr. Symons. This gives us an intimation why the artist is—each within his own limitations—oftenest to be depended upon as a critic; his criticism will be criticism, and not the satisfaction of a suppressed creative wish—which, in most other persons, is apt to interfere fatally.

Before considering what the proper critical reaction of artistic sensibility is, how far criticism is "feeling" and how far "thought," and what sort of "thought" is permitted, it may be instructive to prod a little into that other temperament, so different from Mr. Symons', which issues in generalities such as that quoted near the beginning of this article.

## II

"L'écrivain de style abstrait est presque toujours un sentimental, du moins un sensitif. L'écrivain artiste n'est presque jamais un sentimental, et très rarement un sensitif."—*Le Problème du Style.*

The statement already quoted, that "poetry is the most highly organized form of intellectual activity," may be taken as a specimen of the abstract style in criticism. The confused distinction which exists in most heads between "abstract" and "concrete" is due not so much to a manifest fact of the existence of two types of mind, an abstract and a concrete, as to the existence of another type of mind, the verbal, or philosophic. I, of course, do not imply any general condemnation of philosophy; I am, for the moment, using the word "philosophic" to cover the unscientific ingredients of philosophy; to cover, in fact, the greater part of the philosophic output of the last hundred years. There are two ways in which a word may be "abstract." It may have (the word "activity," for example) a meaning which cannot be grasped by appeal to any of the senses; its apprehension may require a deliberate suppression of analogies of visual or muscular experience, which is none the less an effort of imagination. "Activity" will mean for the trained scientist, if he employ the term, either nothing at all or something still more exact than anything it suggests to us. If we are allowed to accept certain remarks of Pascal and Mr. Bertrand Russell about mathematics, we believe that the mathematician deals with objects—if he will permit us to call them objects—which directly affect his sensibility. And during a good part of history the philosopher endeavoured to deal with objects which he believed to be of the same exactness as the mathematician's. Finally Hegel arrived, and if not perhaps the first, he was certainly the most prodigious exponent of emotional systematization, dealing with his emotions as if they were definite objects which had aroused those emotions. His followers have as a rule taken for granted that words have definite meanings, overlooking the tendency of words to become indefinite emotions. (No one who had not witnessed the event could imagine the conviction in the tone of Professor Eucken as he pounded the table and exclaimed *Was ist Geist? Geist ist...*) If verbalism were confined to professional philosophers, no harm would be done. But their corruption has extended very far. Compare a mediæval theologian or mystic, compare a seventeenth-century preacher, with any "liberal" sermon since Schleiermacher, and you will observe that words have changed their meanings. What they have lost is definite, and what they have gained is indefinite.

The vast accumulations of knowledge—or at least of information—deposited by the nineteenth century have been responsible for an equally vast ignorance. When there is so much to be known, when there are so many fields of knowledge in which the same words are used with different meanings, when every one knows a little about a great many things, it becomes increasingly difficult for anyone to know whether he knows what he is talking about or not. And when we do not know, or when we do not know enough, we tend always to substitute emotions for thoughts. The sentence so frequently quoted in this essay will serve for an example of this process as well as any, and may be profitably contrasted with the opening phrases of the *Posterior Analytics*. Not only all knowledge, but all feeling, is in perception. The inventor of poetry as the most highly organized form of intellectual activity was not engaged in perceiving when he composed this definition; he had nothing to be aware of except his own emotion about "poetry." He was, in fact, absorbed in a very different "activity" not only from that of Mr. Symons, but from that of Aristotle.

Aristotle is a person who has suffered from the adherence of persons who must be regarded less as his disciples than as his sectaries. One must be firmly distrustful of accepting Aristotle in a canonical spirit; this is to lose the whole living force of him. He was primarily a man of not only remarkable but universal intelligence; and universal intelligence means that he could apply his intelligence to anything. The ordinary intelligence is good only for certain classes of objects; a brilliant man of science, if he is interested in poetry at all, may conceive grotesque judgments: like one poet because he reminds him of himself, or another because he expresses emotions which he admires; he may use art, in fact, as the outlet for the egotism which is suppressed in his own speciality. But Aristotle had none of these impure desires to satisfy; in whatever sphere of interest, he looked solely and steadfastly at the object; in his short and broken treatise he provides an eternal example—not of laws, or even of method, for there is no method except to be very intelligent, but of intelligence itself swiftly operating the analysis of sensation to the point of principle and definition.

It is far less Aristotle than Horace who has been the model for criticism up to the nineteenth century. A precept, such as Horace or Boileau gives us, is merely an unfinished analysis. It appears as a law, a rule, because it does not appear in its most general form; it is empirical. When we understand necessity, as Spinoza knew, we are free because we assent. The dogmatic critic, who lays down a rule, who affirms a value, has left his labour incomplete. Such statements may often be justifiable as a saving of time; but in matters of great importance the critic must not coerce, and he must not make judgments of worse and better. He must simply elucidate: the reader will form the correct judgment for himself.

And again, the purely "technical" critic—the critic, that is, who writes to expound some novelty or impart some lesson to practitioners of an art—can be called a critic only in a narrow sense. He may be analysing perceptions and the means for arousing perceptions, but his aim is limited and is not the disinterested exercise of intelligence. The narrowness of the aim makes easier the detection of the merit or feebleness of the work; even of these writers there are very few—so that their "criticism" is of great importance within its limits. So much suffices for Campion. Dryden is far more disinterested; he displays much free intelligence; and yet even Dryden—or any *literary* critic of the seventeenth century—is not quite a free mind, compared, for instance, with such a mind as Rochefoucauld's. There is always a tendency to legislate rather than to inquire, to revise accepted laws, even to overturn, but to reconstruct out of the same material. And the free intelligence is that which is wholly devoted to inquiry.

Coleridge, again, whose natural abilities, and some of whose performances, are probably more remarkable than those of any other modern critic, cannot be estimated as an intelligence completely free. The nature of the restraint in his case is quite different from that which limited the seventeenth-century critics, and is much more personal. Coleridge's metaphysical interest was quite genuine, and was, like most metaphysical interest, an affair of his emotions. But a literary critic should have no emotions except those immediately provoked by a work of art—and these (as I have already hinted) are, when valid, perhaps not to be called emotions at all. Coleridge is apt to take leave of the data of criticism, and arouse the suspicion that he has been diverted into a metaphysical hare-and-hounds. His end does not always appear to be the return to the work of art with improved perception and intensified, because more conscious, enjoyment; his centre of interest changes, his feelings are impure. In the derogatory sense he is more "philosophic" than Aristotle. For everything that Aristotle says illuminates the literature which is the occasion for saying it; but Coleridge only now and then. It is one more instance of the pernicious effect of emotion.

Aristotle had what is called the scientific mind—a mind which, as it is rarely found among scientists except in fragments, might better be called the intelligent mind. For there is no other intelligence than this, and so far as artists and men of letters are intelligent (we may doubt whether the level of intelligence among men of letters is as high as among men of science) their intelligence is of this kind. Sainte-Beuve was a physiologist by training; but it is probable that his mind, like that of the ordinary scientific specialist, was limited in its interest, and that this was not, primarily, an interest in art. If he was a critic, there is no doubt that he was a very good one; but we may conclude that he earned some other name. Of all modern critics, perhaps Remy de Gourmont had most of the general intelligence of Aristotle. An amateur, though an excessively able amateur, in physiology, he combined to a remarkable degree sensitiveness, erudition, sense of fact and sense of history, and generalizing power.

We assume the gift of a superior sensibility. And for sensibility wide and profound reading does not mean merely a more extended pasture. There is not merely an increase of understanding, leaving the original acute impression unchanged. The new impressions modify the impressions received from the objects already known. An impression needs to be constantly refreshed by new impressions in order that it may persist at all; it needs to take its place in a system of impressions. And this system tends to become articulate in a generalized statement of literary beauty.

There are, for instance, many scattered lines and tercets in the *Divine Comedy* which are capable of transporting even a quite uninitiated reader, just sufficiently acquainted with the roots of the language to decipher the meaning, to an impression of overpowering beauty. This impression may be so deep that no subsequent study and understanding will intensify it. But at this point the impression is emotional; the reader in the ignorance which we postulate is unable to distinguish the poetry from an emotional state aroused in himself by the poetry, a state which may be merely an indulgence of his own emotions. The poetry may be an accidental stimulus. The end of the enjoyment of poetry is a pure contemplation from which all the accidents of personal emotion are removed; thus we aim to see the object as it really is and find a meaning for the words of Arnold. And without a labour which is largely a labour of the intelligence, we are unable to attain that stage of vision *amor intellectualis Dei.*

Such considerations, cast in this general form, may appear commonplaces. But I believe that it is always opportune to call attention to the torpid superstition that appreciation is one thing, and "intellectual" criticism something else. Appreciation in popular psychology is one faculty, and criticism another, an arid cleverness building theoretical scaffolds upon one's own perceptions or those of others. On the contrary, the true generalization is not something superposed upon an accumulation of perceptions; the perceptions do not, in a really appreciative mind, accumulate as a mass, but form themselves as a structure; and criticism is the statement in language of this structure; it is a development of sensibility. The bad criticism, on the other hand, is that which is nothing but an expression of emotion. And emotional people—such as stockbrokers, politicians, men of science—and a few people who pride themselves on being unemotional—detest or applaud great writers such as Spinoza or Stendhal because of their "frigidity."

The writer of the present essay once committed himself to the statement that "The poetic critic is criticizing poetry in order to create poetry." He is now inclined to believe that the "historical" and the "philosophical" critics had better be called historians and philosophers quite simply. As for the rest, there are merely various degrees of intelligence. It is fatuous to say that criticism is for the sake of "creation" or creation for the sake of criticism. It is also fatuous to assume that there are ages of criticism and ages of creativeness, as if by plunging ourselves into intellectual darkness we were in better hope of finding spiritual light. The two directions of sensibility are complementary; and as sensibility is rare, unpopular, and desirable, it is to be expected that the critic and the creative artist should frequently be the same person.

# IMPERFECT CRITICS

## Swinburne as Critic

THREE conclusions at least issue from the perusal of Swinburne's critical essays: Swinburne had mastered his material, was more inward with the Tudor-Stuart dramatists than any man of pure letters before or since; he is a more reliable guide to them than Hazlitt, Coleridge, or Lamb; and his perception of relative values is almost always correct. Against these merits we may oppose two objections: the style is the prose style of Swinburne, and the content is not, in an exact sense, criticism. The faults of style are, of course, personal; the tumultuous outcry of adjectives, the headstrong rush of undisciplined sentences, are the index to the impatience and perhaps laziness of a disorderly mind. But the style has one positive merit: it allows us to know that Swinburne was writing not to establish a critical reputation, not to instruct a docile public, but as a poet his notes upon poets whom he admired. And whatever our opinion of Swinburne's verse, the notes upon poets by a poet of Swinburne's dimensions must be read with attention and respect.

In saying that Swinburne's essays have the value of notes of an important poet upon important poets, we must place a check upon our expectancy. He read everything, and he read with the single interest in finding literature. The critics of the romantic period were pioneers, and exhibit the fallibility of discoverers. The selections of Lamb are a successful effort of good taste, but anyone who has referred to them after a thorough reading of any of the poets included must have found that some of the best passages—which must literally have stared Lamb in the face—are omitted, while sometimes others of less value are included. Hazlitt, who committed himself to the judgment that the *Maid's Tragedy* is one of the poorest of Beaumont and Fletcher's plays, has no connected message to deliver. Coleridge's remarks—too few and scattered—have permanent truth; but on some of the greatest names he passes no remark, and of some of the best plays was perhaps ignorant or ill-informed. But compared with Swinburne, Coleridge writes much more as a poet might be expected to write about poets. Of Massinger's verse Swinburne says:

> It is more serviceable, more businesslike, more eloquently practical, and more rhetorically effusive—but never effusive beyond the bounds of effective rhetoric—than the style of any Shakespearean or of any Jonsonian dramatist.

It is impossible to tell whether Webster would have found the style of Massinger more "serviceable" than his own for the last act of the *White Devil*, and indeed difficult to decide what "serviceable" here means; but it is quite clear what Coleridge means when he says that Massinger's style

> is much more easily constructed [than Shakespeare's], and may be more successfully adopted by writers in the present day.

Coleridge is writing as a professional with his eye on the technique. I do not know from what writing of Coleridge Swinburne draws the assertion that "Massinger often deals in exaggerated passion," but in the essay from which Swinburne quotes elsewhere Coleridge merely speaks of the "unnaturally irrational passions," a phrase much more defensible. Upon the whole, the two poets are in harmony upon the subject of Massinger; and although Coleridge has said more in five pages, and said it more clearly, than Swinburne in thirty-nine, the essay of Swinburne is by no means otiose: it is more stimulating than Coleridge's, and the stimulation is never misleading. With all his superlatives, his judgment, if carefully scrutinized, appears temperate and just.

With all his justness of judgment, however, Swinburne is an appreciator and not a critic. In the whole range of literature covered, Swinburne makes hardly more than two judgments which can be reversed or even questioned: one, that Lyly is insignificant as a dramatist, and the other, that Shirley was probably unaffected by Webster. The *Cardinal* is not a cast of the *Duchess of Malfi*, certainly; but when Shirley wrote

> the mist is risen, and there's none
> To steer my wandering bark. *(Dies.)*

he was probably affected by

> My soul, like to a ship in a black storm,
> Is driven, I know not whither.

Swinburne's judgment is generally sound, his taste sensitive and discrim-
inating. And we cannot say that his thinking is faulty or perverse—up to
the point at which it is thinking. But Swinburne stops thinking just at the
moment when we are most zealous to go on. And this arrest, while it does
not vitiate his work, makes it an introduction rather than a statement.

We are aware, after the *Contemporaries of Shakespeare* and the *Age of
Shakespeare* and the books on Shakespeare and Jonson, that there is something unsatisfactory in the way in which Swinburne was interested in
these people; we suspect that his interest was never articulately formulated
in his mind or consciously directed to any purpose. He makes his way, or
loses it, between two paths of definite direction. He might as a poet have
concentrated his attention upon the technical problems solved or tackled
by these men; he might have traced for us the development of blank verse
from Sackville to the mature Shakespeare, and its degeneration from
Shakespeare to Milton. Or he might have studied through the literature
to the mind of that century; he might, by dissection and analysis, have
helped us to some insight into the feeling and thought which we seem to
have left so far away. In either case, you would have had at least the
excitement of following the movements of an important mind groping
towards important conclusions. As it is, there are to be no conclusions,
except that Elizabethan literature is very great, and that you can have
pleasure and even ecstasy from it, because a sensitive poetic talent has
had the experience. One is in risk of becoming fatigued by a hubbub that
does not march; the drum is beaten, but the procession does not advance.

If, for example, Swinburne's interest was in poetry, why devote an essay
to Brome? "The opening scene of the *Sparagus Garden,* says Swinburne, "is
as happily humorous and as vividly natural as that of any more famous
comedy." The scene is both humorous and natural. Brome deserves to be
more read than he is, and first of all to be more accessible than he is. But
Swinburne ought to suggest or imply (I do not say impose) a reason for
reading the *Sparagus Garden* or the *Antipodes,* more sufficient than any he
has provided. No doubt such reason could be found.

When it is a matter of pronouncing judgment between two poets,
Swinburne is almost unerring. He is certainly right in putting Webster
above Tourneur, Tourneur above Ford, and Ford above Shirley. He
weighs accurately the good and evil in Fletcher: he perceives the essential theatricality, but his comparison of the *Faithful Shepherdess* with *Comus*
is a judgment no word of which can be improved upon:

> The difference between this poem [*i.e.* the *Faithful Shepherdess*]
> and Milton's exquisitely imitative *Comus* is the difference between a

rose with a leaf or two faded or falling, but still fragrant and radiant, and the faultless but scentless reproduction of a rose in academic wax for the admiration and imitation of such craftsmen as must confine their ambition to the laurels of a college or the plaudits of a school.

In the longest and most important essay in the *Contemporaries of Shakespeare*, the essay on Chapman, there are many such sentences of sound judgment forcibly expressed. The essay is the best we have on that great poet. It communicates the sense of dignity and mass which we receive from Chapman. But it also illustrates Swinburne's infirmities. Swinburne was not tormented by the restless desire to penetrate to the heart and marrow of a poet, any more than he was tormented by the desire to render the finest shades of difference and resemblance between several poets. Chapman is a difficult author, as Swinburne says; he is far more difficult than Jonson, to whom he bears only a superficial likeness. He is difficult beyond his obscurity. He is difficult partly through his possession of a quality comparatively deficient in Jonson, but which was nevertheless a quality of the age. It is strange that Swinburne should have hinted at a similarity to Jonson and not mentioned a far more striking affinity of Chapman's—that is, Donne. The man who wrote

> Guise, O my lord, how shall I cast from me
> The bands and coverts hindering me from thee?
> The garment or the cover of the mind
> The humane soul is; of the soul, the spirit
> The proper robe is; of the spirit, the blood;
> And of the blood, the body is the shroud

and

> Nothing is made of nought, of all things made,
> Their abstract being a dream but of a shade,

is unquestionably kin to Donne. The quality in question is not peculiar to Donne and Chapman. In common with the greatest—Marlowe, Webster, Tourneur, and Shakespeare—they had a quality of sensuous thought, or of thinking through the senses, or of the senses thinking, of which the exact formula remains to be defined. If you look for it in Shelley or Beddoes, both of whom in very different ways recaptured something of the Elizabethan inspiration, you will not find it, though you may find other qualities instead. There is a trace of it only in Keats, and, derived from a different source, in Rossetti. You will not find it in the *Duke of Gandia*. Swinburne's essay would have been all the better if he had applied himself to the solution of problems like this.

He did not apply himself to this sort of problem because this was not the sort of problem that interested him. The author of Swinburne's critical essays is also the author of Swinburne's verse: if you hold the opinion that Swinburne was a very great poet, you can hardly deny him the title of a great critic. There is the same curious mixture of qualities to produce Swinburne's own effect, resulting in the same blur, which only the vigour of the colours fixes. His great merit as a critic is really one which, like many signal virtues, can be stated so simply as to appear flat. It is that he was sufficiently interested in his subject-matter and knew quite enough about it; and this is a rare combination in English criticism. Our critics are often interested in extracting something from their subject which is not fairly in it. And it is because this elementary virtue is so rare that Swinburne must take a very respectable place as a critic. Critics are often interested—but not quite in the nominal subject, often in something a little beside the point; they are often learned—but not quite to the point either. (Swinburne knew some of the plays almost by heart.) Can this particular virtue at which we have glanced be attributed to Walter Pater? or to Professor Bradley? or to Swinburne's editor?

### A Romantic Aristocrat

It is impossible to overlook the merits of scholarship and criticism exhibited by George Wyndham's posthumous book, and it is impossible to deal with the book purely on its merits of scholarship and criticism. To attempt to do so would in the first place be unfair, as the book is a posthumous work, and posthumous books demand some personal attention to their writers. This book is a collection of essays and addresses, arranged in their present order by Mr. Whibley; they were intended by their author to be remodelled into a volume on "romantic literature"; they move from an ingenious search for the date of the beginning of Romanticism, through the French and English Renaissance, to Sir Walter Scott. In the second place, these essays represent the literary work of a man who gained his chief distinction in political life. In the third place, this man stands for a type, an English type. The type is interesting and will probably become extinct. It is natural, therefore, that our primary interest in the essays should be an interest in George Wyndham.

Mr. Charles Whibley, in an introduction the tone of which is well suited to the matter, has several sentences which throw light on Wyndham's personality. What issues with surprising clearness from Mr. Whibley's sketch is the unity of Wyndham's mind, the identity of his mind as it engaged in apparently unrelated occupations. Wyndham left Eton for the army; in barracks he "taught himself Italian, and filled his leisure with the reading of history and poetry." After this Coldstream culture there was a campaign in Egypt; later, service in South Africa accompanied by a copy of Virgil. There was a career in the Commons, a conspicuous career as Irish Secretary. Finally, there was a career as a landowner—2400 acres. And throughout these careers George Wyndham went on not only accumulating books but reading them, and occasionally writing about them. He was a man of character, a man of energy. Mr. Whibley is quite credible when he says:

> Literature was for him no parergon, no mere way of escape from politics. If he was an amateur in feeling, he was a craftsman in execution;

and, more significantly,

> With the same zest that he read and discoursed upon *A Winter's Tale* or *Troilus and Cressida,* he rode to hounds, or threw himself with a kind of fury into a "point to point," or made a speech at the hustings, or sat late in the night talking with a friend.

From these and other sentences we chart the mind of George Wyndham, and the key to its topography is the fact that his literature and his politics and his country life are one and the same thing. They are not in separate compartments, they are one career. Together they made up his world: literature, politics, riding to hounds. In the real world these things have nothing to do with each other. But we cannot believe that George Wyndham lived in the real world. And this is implied in Mr. Whibley's remark that:

> George Wyndham was by character and training a romantic. He looked with wonder upon the world as upon a fairyland.

Here is the manifestation of type.

There must probably be conceded to history a few "many-sided" men. Perhaps Leonardo da Vinci was such. George Wyndham was not a man on the scale of Leonardo, and his writings give a very different effect

from Leonardo's notebooks. Leonardo turned to art or science, and each
was what it was and not another thing. But Leonardo was Leonardo: he
had no father to speak of, he was hardly a citizen, and he had no stake in
the community. He lived in no fairyland, but his mind went out and became
a part of things. George Wyndham was Gentry. He was chivalrous, the
world was an adventure of himself. It is characteristic that on embarking
as a subaltern for Egypt he wrote enthusiastically:

> I do not suppose that any expedition since the days of Roman
> governors of provinces has started with such magnificence; we
> might have been Antony going to Egypt in a purple-sailed galley.

This is precisely the spirit which animates his appreciation of the
Elizabethans and of Walter Scott; which guides him toward Hakluyt
and North. Wyndham was enthusiastic, he was a Romantic, he was an
Imperialist, and he was quite naturally a literary pupil of W. E. Henley.
Wyndham was a scholar, but his scholarship is incidental; he was a good
critic, within the range allowed him by his enthusiasms; but it is neither
as Scholar nor as Critic that we can criticize him. We can criticize his
writings only as the expression of this peculiar English type, the aristo-
crat, the Imperialist, the Romantic, riding to hounds across his prose,
looking with wonder upon the world as upon a fairyland.

Because he belongs to this type, Wyndham wrote enthusiastically and
well about North's Plutarch. The romance of the ancient world becomes
more romantic in the idiomatic prose of North; the heroes are not merely
Greek and Roman heroes, but Elizabethan heroes as well; the romantic
fusion allured Wyndham. The charms of North could not be expounded
more delightfully, more seductively, with more gusto, than they are in
Wyndham's essay. He appreciates the battles, the torchlight, the "dead
sound" of drums, the white, worn face of Cicero in his flight peering from
his litter; he appreciates the sharp brusque phrase of North: "he roundly
trussed them up and hung them by their necks." And Wyndham is
learned. Here, as in his essays on the Pléiade and Shakespeare, the man
has read everything, with a labour that only whets his enjoyment of the
best. There are two defects: a lack of balance and a lack of critical profundity. The lack of balance peeps through Wyndham's condemnation of
an obviously inferior translation of Plutarch: "He dedicated the superfluity of his leisure to enjoyment, and used his Lamia," says the bad translator. North: "he took pleasure of Lamia." Wyndham makes a set upon the
bad translator. But he forgets that "dedicated the superfluity of his

leisure" is such a phrase as Gibbon would have warmed to life and wit, and that a history, in the modern sense, could not be written in the style of North. Wyndham forgets, in short, that it is not, in the end, periods and traditions but individual men who write great prose. For Wyndham is himself a period and a tradition.

The lack of balance is to be suspected elsewhere. Wyndham *likes* the best, but he likes a good deal. There is no conclusive evidence that he realized all the difference, the gulf of difference between lines like:

> En l'an trentiesme de mon aage
> Que toutes mes hontes j'ay beues;

and even the very best of Ronsard or Bellay, such as:

> Le temps s'en va, le temps s'en va, madame;
> Las! le temps, non, mais nous nous en allons
> Et tost serons estendus sous la lame.

We should not gather from Wyndham's essay that the *Phœnix and Turtle* is a great poem, far finer than *Venus and Adonis;* but what he says about *Venus and Adonis* is worth reading, for Wyndham is very sharp in perceiving the neglected beauties of the second-rate. There is nothing to show the gulf of difference between Shakespeare's sonnets and those of any other Elizabethan. Wyndham overrates Sidney, and in his references to Elizabethan writings on the theory of poetry omits mention of the essay by Campion, an abler and more daring though less common-sense study than Daniel's. He speaks a few words for Drayton, but has not noticed that the only good lines (with the exception of one sonnet which may be an accident) in Drayton's dreary sequence of "Ideas" occur when Drayton drops his costume for a moment and talks in terms of actuality:

> Lastly, mine eyes amazedly have seen
> Essex' great fall; Tyrone his peace to gain;
> The quiet end of that long-living queen;
> The king's fair entry, and our peace with Spain.

More important than the lack of balance is the lack of critical analysis. Wyndham had, as was indicated, a gusto for the Elizabethans. His essay on the Poems of Shakespeare contains an extraordinary amount of information. There is some interesting gossip about Mary Fitton and a good anecdote of Sir William Knollys. But Wyndham misses what is the cardinal point in criticizing the Elizabethans: we cannot grasp them, understand them, without understanding of the pathology of rhetoric. Rhetoric, a particular form of rhetoric, was endemic, it pervaded the whole organism; the healthy as well as the morbid tissues were built up on it. We cannot grapple with even the simplest and most conversational lines in Tudor and early Stuart drama without having diagnosed the rhetoric in the sixteenth and seventeenth-century mind. Even when we come across lines like:

> There's a plumber laying pipes in my guts, it scalds,

we must not allow ourselves to forget the rhetorical basis any more than when we read:

> Come, let us march against the powers of heaven
> And set black streamers in the firmament
> To signify the slaughter of the gods.

An understanding of Elizabethan rhetoric is as essential to the appreciation of Elizabethan literature as an understanding of Victorian sentiment is essential to the appreciation of Victorian literature and of George Wyndham.

Wyndham was a Romantic; the only cure for Romanticism is to analyse it. What is permanent and good in Romanticism is curiosity—

> . . . l' ardore
> Ch' i' ebbe a divenir del mondo esperto
> E degli vizii umani e del valore—

a curiosity which recognizes that any life, if accurately and profoundly penetrated, is interesting and always strange. Romanticism is a short cut to the strangeness without the reality, and it leads its disciples only back upon themselves. George Wyndham had curiosity, but he employed it romantically, not to penetrate the real world, but to complete the varied features of the world he made for himself. It would be of interest to divagate from literature to politics and inquire to what extent Romanticism is incorporate in Imperialism; to inquire to what extent Romanticism has possessed the imagination of Imperialists, and to what extent it was made use of by Disraeli. But this is quite another matter: there may be a good deal to be said for Romanticism in life, there is no place for it in letters. Not that we need conclude that a man of George Wyndham's antecedents and traditions must inevitably be a Romanticist writer. But this is the case when such a man plants himself firmly in his awareness of caste, when he says "The gentry must not abdicate." In politics this may be an admirable formula. It will not do in literature. The Arts insist that a man shall dispose of all that he has, even of his family tree, and follow art alone. For they require that a man be not a member of a family or of a caste or of a party or of a coterie, but simply and solely himself. A man like Wyndham brings several virtues into literature. But there is only one man better and more uncommon than the patrician, and that is the Individual.

### The Local Flavour

In a world which is chiefly occupied with the task of keeping up to date with itself, it is a satisfaction to know that there is at least one man who has not only read but enjoyed, and not only enjoyed but read, such authors as Petronius and Herondas. That is Mr. Charles Whibley, and there are two statements to make about him: that he is not a critic, and that he is something which is almost as rare, if not quite as precious. He has apparently read and enjoyed a great deal of English literature, and the part of it that he has most enjoyed is the literature of the great ages, the sixteenth and seventeenth centuries. We may opine that Mr. Whibley has not uttered a single important original judgment upon any of this literature. On the other hand, how many have done so? Mr. Whibley is not a critic of men or of books; but he convinces us that if we read the books that he has read we should find them as delightful as he has found them; and if we read them we can form our own opinions. And if he has not the balance of the critic, he has some other equipoise of his own. It is partly that his tastes are not puritanical, that he can talk about Restoration dramatists and others without apologizing for their "indecency"; it is partly his sense for the best local and temporal flavours; it is partly his healthy appetite.

A combination of non-critical, rather than uncritical, qualities made Mr. Whibley the most appropriate person in the world for the work by which he is best known. We should be more grateful for the "Tudor Translations Series" if we could find copies to be bought, and if we could afford to buy them when we found them. But that is not Mr. Whibley's fault. The introductions which he wrote for some of the translators are all that such introductions should be. His Urquhart's *Rabelais* contains all the irrelevant information about that writer which is what is wanted to stimulate a taste for him. After reading the introduction, to read Urquhart was the only pleasure in life. And therefore, in a country destitute of living criticism, Mr. Whibley is a useful person: for the first thing is that English literature should be read at all. The few people who talk intelligently about Stendhal and Flaubert and James know this; but the larger number of people who skim the conversation of the former do not know enough of English literature to be even insular. There are two ways in which a writer may lead us to profit by the work of dead writers. One is by isolating the essential, by pointing out the most intense in various kinds and separating it from the accidents of environment. This method is helpful only to the more intelligent people, who are capable of a unique enjoyment of perfect expression, and it concentrates on the very best in any art. The other method, that of Mr. Whibley, is to communicate a taste for the period—and for the best of the period so far as it is of that period. That is not very easy either. For a pure journalist will not know any period well enough; a pure dilettante will know it too egotistically, as a fashion of his own. Mr. Whibley is really interested; and he has escaped, without any programme of revolt, from the present century into those of Tudor and Stuart. He escapes, and perhaps leads others, by virtue of a taste which is not exactly a literary taste.

The "Tudor Translations" form part of a pronounced taste. Some are better written than others. There is, of course, a world of difference—of which Mr. Whibley is perhaps unaware—between even Florio and his original. The French of Montaigne is a mature language, and the English of Florio's living translation is not. Montaigne could be translated into the English of his time, but a similar work could not have been written in it. But as the English language matured it lost something that Florio and all his inferior colleagues had, and that they had in common with the language of Montaigne. It was not only the language, but the time. The prose of that age had life, a life to which later ages could not add, from which they could only take away. You find the same life, the same abundance, in Montaigne and Brantôme, the alteration in Rochefoucauld as in Hobbes, the desiccation in the classic prose of both languages, in Voltaire and in Gibbon. Only, the French was originally richer and more mature—already in Joinville and Commines—and we have no prose to compare with Montaigne and Rabelais. If Mr. Whibley had analysed this vitality, and told us why Holland and Underdowne, Nashe and Martin Marprelate are still worth reading, then he could have shown us how to recognize this quality when it, or something like it, appears in our own lifetime. But Mr. Whibley is not an analyst. His taste, even, becomes less certain as he fixes it on individuals within his period. On Surrey's blank verse he is feeble; he does not even give Surrey the credit of having anticipated some of Tennyson's best effects. He has no praise for Golding, quite one of the best of the verse translators; he apologizes for him by saying that Ovid demands no strength or energy! There is strength and energy, at least, in Marlowe's *Amores*. And he omits mention of Gawain Douglas, who, though he wrote in Scots, was surely a "Tudor" translator. Characteristically, Mr. Whibley praises Chapman because

> it gives proof of an abounding life, a quenchless energy. There is a grandeur and spirit in Chapman's rendering, not unworthy the original . . .

This is commonplace, and it is uncritical. And a critic would not use so careless a phrase as "Tasso's masterpiece." The essay on Congreve does not add much to our understanding:

> And so he set upon the boards a set of men and women of quick brains and cynical humours, who talked with the brilliance and rapidity wherewith the finished swordsman fences.

We have heard of this conversation like fencing before. And the suspicion is in our breast that Mr. Whibley might admire George Meredith. The essay on Ralegh gives still less. The reality of that pleasing pirate and monopolist has escaped, and only the national hero is left. And yet Ralegh, and Swift, and Congreve, and the underworld of sixteenth and seventeenth-century letters, are somehow kept alive by what Mr. Whibley says of them.

Accordingly, Mr. Whibley does not disappear in the jungle of journalism and false criticism; he deserves a "place upon the shelves" of those who care for English literature. He has the first requisite of a critic: interest in his subject, and ability to communicate an interest in it. His defects are both of intellect and feeling. He has no dissociative faculty. There were very definite vices and definite shortcomings and immaturities in the literature he admires; and as he is not the person to tell us of the vices and shortcomings, he is not the person to lay before us the work of absolutely the finest quality. He exercises neither of the tools of the critic: comparison and analysis. He has not the austerity of passion which can detect unerringly the transition from work of eternal intensity to work that is merely beautiful, and from work that is beautiful to work that is merely charming. For the critic needs to be able not only to saturate himself in the spirit and the fashion of a time—the local flavour—but also to separate himself suddenly from it in appreciation of the highest creative work.

And he needs something else that Mr. Whibley lacks: a creative interest, a focus upon the immediate future. The important critic is the person who is absorbed in the present problems of art, and who wishes to bring the forces of the past to bear upon the solution of these problems. If the critic consider Congreve, for instance, he will have always at the back of his mind the question: What has Congreve got that is pertinent to our dramatic art? Even if he is solely engaged in trying to understand Congreve, this will make all the difference: inasmuch as to understand anything is to understand from a point of view. Most critics have some creative interest—it may be, instead of an interest in any art, an interest (like Mr. Paul More's) in morals. These remarks were introduced only to assist in giving the books of Mr. Whibley a place, a particular but unticketed place, neither with criticism, nor with history, nor with plain journalism; and the trouble would not have been taken if the books were not thought to be worth placing.

## A Note on the American Critic

This gallery of critics is not intended to be in any sense complete. But having dealt with three English writers of what may be called critical prose, one's mind becomes conscious of the fact that they have something in common, and, trying to perceive more clearly what this community is, and suspecting that it is a national quality, one is impelled to meditate upon the strongest contrast possible. Hence these comments upon two American critics and one French critic, which would not take exactly this form without the contrast at which I have hinted.

Mr. Paul More is the author of a number of volumes which he perhaps hopes will break the record of mass established by the complete works of Sainte-Beuve. The comparison with Sainte-Beuve is by no means trivial, for Mr. More, and Professor Irving Babbitt also, are admirers of the voluminous Frenchman. Not only are they admirers, but their admiration is perhaps a clue both to much of their merit and to some of their defects. In the first place, both of these writers have given much more attention to French criticism, to the study of French standards of writing and of thought, than any of the notable English critics since Arnold; they are therefore much nearer to the European current, although they exhibit faults which are definitely transatlantic and which definitely keep them out of it. The French influence is traceable in their devotion to ideas and their interest in problems of art and life as problems which exist and can be handled apart from their relations to the critic's private temperament. With Swinburne, the criticism of Elizabethan literature has the interest

of a passion, it has the interest for us of any writing by an intellectual man
who is genuinely moved by certain poetry. Swinburne's intelligence is not
defective, it is impure. There are few ideas in Swinburne's critical writings which stand forth luminous with an independent life of their own, so
true that one forgets the author in the statement. Swinburne's words must
always be referred back to Swinburne himself. And if literature is to
Swinburne merely a passion, we are tempted to say that to George
Wyndham it was a hobby, and to Mr. Whibley almost a charming showman's show (we are charmed by the urbanity of the showman). The two
latter have gusto, but gusto is no equivalent for taste; it depends too much
upon the appetite and the digestion of the feeder. And with one or two
other writers, whom I have not had occasion to discuss, literature is not
so much a collection of valuable porcelain as an institution—accepted, that
is to say, with the same gravity as the establishments of Church and State.
That is, in other words, the essentially uncritical attitude. In all of these
attitudes the English critic is the victim of his temperament. He may
acquire great erudition, but erudition easily becomes a hobby; it is use-
less unless it enables us to see literature all round, to detach it from ourselves, to reach a state of pure contemplation.

Now Mr. More and Mr. Babbitt have endeavoured to establish a criticism which should be independent of temperament. This is in itself a
considerable merit. But at this point Mr. More particularly has been led
astray, oddly enough, by his guide Sainte-Beuve. Neither Mr. More nor
Sainte-Beuve is primarily interested in art. Of the latter M. Benda has
well observed that

> on sait—et c'est certainement un des grands éléments de son
> succès—combien d'études l'illustre critique consacre à des auteurs
> dont l'importance littéraire est quasi nulle (femmes, magistrats,
> courtisans, militaires), mais dont les écrits lui sont une occasion de
> pourtraiturer une âme; combien volontiers, pour les maîtres, il s'at-
> tache à leurs productions secondaires, notes, brouillons, lettres
> intimes, plutôt qu'à leurs grandes œuvres, souvent beaucoup moins
> expressives, en effet, de leur psychologie.

Mr. More is not, like Sainte-Beuve, primarily interested in psychology or
in human beings; Mr. More is primarily a moralist, which is a worthy and
serious thing to be. The trouble with Mr. More is that you cannot disperse
a theory or point of view of morals over a vast number of essays on a
great variety of important figures in literature, unless you can give some
more particular interest as well. Sainte-Beuve has his particularized
interest in human beings; another critic—say Remy de Gourmont—may

have something to say always about the art of a writer which will make our enjoyment of that writer more conscious and more intelligent. But the pure moralist in letters—the moralist is useful to the creator as well as the reader of poetry—must be more concise, for we must have the pleasure of inspecting the beauty of his structure. And here M. Julien Benda has a great advantage over Mr. More; his thought may be less profound, but it has more formal beauty.

Mr. Irving Babbitt, who shares so many of the ideals and opinions of Mr. More that their names must be coupled, has expressed his thought more abstractly and with more form, and is free from a mystical impulse which occasionally gets out of Mr. More's hand. He appears, more clearly than Mr. More, and certainly more clearly than any critic of equal authority in America or England, to perceive Europe as a whole; he has the cosmopolitan mind and tendency to seek the centre. His few books are important, and would be more important if he preached of discipline in a more disciplined style. Although he also is an admirer of Sainte-Beuve, he would probably subscribe to this admirable paragraph of Othenin d'Haussonville:[1]

> Il y a une beauté littéraire, impersonnelle en quelque sorte, parfaitement distincte de l'auteur lui-même et de son organisation, beauté qui a sa raison d'être et ses lois, dont la critique est tenue de rendre compte. Et si la critique considère cette tâche comme au-dessous d'elle, si c'est affaire à la rhétorique et à ce que Sainte-Beuve appelle dédaigneusement les Quintilien, alors la rhetorique a du bon et les Quintilien ne sont pas à dédaigner.

There may be several critics in England who would applaud this notion; there are very few who show any evidence of its apprehension in their writings. But Mr. More and Mr. Babbitt, whatever their actual tastes, and although they are not primarily occupied with art, are on the side of the artist. And the side of the artist is not the side which in England is often associated with critical writing. As Mr. More has pointed out in an interesting essay, there is a vital weakness in Arnold's definition of criticism as "the disinterested endeavour to know the best that is known and thought in the world, irrespectively of practice, politics, and everything of the kind." The "disinterested endeavour to know" is only a prerequisite of the *critic,* and is not *criticism,* which may be the result of such an endeavour.

---

[1] *Revue des Deux Mondes,* fevr. 1875, quoted by Benda, *Belphégor,* p. 140.

Arnold states the work of the critic merely in terms of the personal ideal, an ideal for oneself—and an ideal for oneself is not disinterested. Here Arnold is the Briton rather than the European.

Mr. More indicates his own attitude in praising those whom he elevates to the position of masters of criticism:

> If they deal much with the criticism of literature, this is because in literature more manifestly than anywhere else life displays its infinitely varied motives and results; and their practice is always to render literature itself more consciously a criticism of life.

"Criticism of life" is a facile phrase, and at most only represents one aspect of great literature, if it does not assign to the term "criticism" itself a generality which robs it of precision. Mr. More has, it seems to me, in this sentence just failed to put his finger on the right seriousness of great literary art: the seriousness which we find in Villon's *Testament* and which is conspicuously absent from *In Memoriam*; or the seriousness which controls *Amos Barton* and not *The Mill on the Floss*.

It is a pity that Mr. More does not write a little oftener about the great literary artists, it is a pity that he takes the reputations of the world too solemnly. This is probably due in part to remoteness in space from the European centre. But it must be observed that English solemnity and American solemnity are very different. I do not propose to analyse the difference (it would be a valuable chapter in social history); the American solemnity, it is enough to say, is more primitive, more academic, more like that of the German professor. But it is not the fault of Mr. More or Mr. Babbitt that the culture of ideas has only been able to survive in America in the unfavourable atmosphere of the university.

### The French Intelligence

As the inspection of types of English irresistibly provoked a glance at two American critics, so the inspection of the latter leads our attention to the French. M. Julien Benda has the formal beauty which the American critics lack, and a close affinity to them in point of view. He restricts himself, perhaps, to a narrower field of ideas, but within that field he manipulates the ideas with a very exceptional cogency and clarity. To notice his last book *(Belphégor: essai sur l'esthétique de la présente société française)* would be to quote from it. M. Benda is not like Remy de Gourmont, the critical consciousness of a generation, he could not supply the conscious formulas of a sensibility in process of formation; he is rather the ideal scavenger of the rubbish of our time. Much of his analysis of the decadence of contemporary French society could be applied to London, although differences are observable from his diagnosis.

> Quant à la société en elle-même, on peut prévoir que ce soin qu'elle met à éprouver de l'émoi par l'art, devenant cause à son tour, y rendra la soif de ce plaisir de plus en plus intense, l'application à la satisfaire de plus en plus jalouse et plus perfectionnée. On entrevoit le jour où la bonne société française repudiera encore le peu qu'elle supporte aujourd'hui d'idées et d'organisation dans l'art, et ne se passionera plus que pour des gestes de comédiens, pour des impressions de femmes ou d'enfants, pour des rugissements de lyriques, pour des extases de fanatiques . . .

Almost the only person who has ever figured in England and attempted a task at all similar to that of M. Benda is Matthew Arnold. Matthew Arnold was intelligent, and by so much difference as the presence of one intelligent man makes, our age is inferior to that of Arnold. But what an advantage a man like M. Benda has over Arnold. It is not simply that he has a critical tradition behind him, and that Arnold is using a language which constantly tempts the user away from dispassionate exposition into sarcasm and diatribe, a language less fitted for criticism than the English of the eighteenth century. It is that the follies and stupidities of the French, no matter how base, express themselves in the form of ideas—Bergsonism itself is an intellectual construction, and the mondaines who attended lectures at the College de France were in a sense using their minds. A man of ideas needs ideas, or pseudo-ideas, to fight against. And Arnold lacked the active resistance which is necessary to keep a mind at its sharpest.

A society in which a mind like M. Benda's can exercise itself, and in which there are persons like M. Benda, is one which facilitates the task of the creative artist. M. Benda cannot be attached, like Gourmont, to any creative group. He does not wholly partake in that "conscious creation of the field of the present out of the past" which Mr. More considers to be part of the work of the critic. But in analysing the maladies of the second-rate or corrupt literature of the time he makes the labour of the creative artist lighter. The Charles Louis Philippes of English literature are never done with, because there is no one to kill their reputations; we still hear that George Meredith is a master of prose, or even a profound philosopher. The creative artist in England finds himself compelled, or at least tempted, to spend much of his time and energy in criticism that he might reserve for the perfecting of his proper work: simply because there is no one else to do it.

# TRADITION AND THE INDIVIDUAL TALENT

## I

IN English writing we seldom speak of tradition, though we occasionally apply its name in deploring its absence. We cannot refer to "the tradition" or to "a tradition"; at most, we employ the adjective in saying that the poetry of So-and-so is "traditional" or even "too traditional." Seldom, perhaps, does the word appear except in a phrase of censure. If otherwise, it is vaguely approbative, with the implication, as to the work approved, of some pleasing archæological reconstruction. You can hardly make the word agreeable to English ears without this comfortable reference to the reassuring science of archæology.

Certainly the word is not likely to appear in our appreciations of living or dead writers. Every nation, every race, has not only its own creative, but its own critical turn of mind; and is even more oblivious of the shortcomings and limitations of its critical habits than of those of its creative genius. We know, or think we know, from the enormous mass of critical writing that has appeared in the French language the critical method or habit of the French; we only conclude (we are such unconscious people) that the French are "more critical" than we, and sometimes even plume ourselves a little with the fact, as if the French were the less spontaneous. Perhaps they are; but we might remind ourselves that criticism is as inevitable as breathing, and that we should be none the worse for articulating what passes in our minds when we read a book and feel an emotion about it, for criticizing our own minds in their work of criticism. One of the facts that might come to light in this process is our tendency to insist, when we praise a poet, upon those aspects of his work in which he least resembles anyone else. In these aspects or parts of his work we pretend to find what is individual, what is the peculiar essence of the man. We dwell with satisfaction upon the poet's difference from his predecessors, especially his immediate predecessors; we endeavour to find something that can be isolated in order to be enjoyed. Whereas if we approach a poet

27

without his prejudice we shall often find that not only the best, but the most individual parts of his work may be those in which the dead poets, his ancestors, assert their immortality most vigorously. And I do not mean the impressionable period of adolescence, but the period of full maturity.

Yet if the only form of tradition, of handing down, consisted in following the ways of the immediate generation before us in a blind or timid adherence to its successes, "tradition" should positively be discouraged. We have seen many such simple currents soon lost in the sand; and novelty is better than repetition. Tradition is a matter of much wider significance. It cannot be inherited, and if you want it you must obtain it by great labour. It involves, in the first place, the historical sense, which we may call nearly indispensable to anyone who would continue to be a poet beyond his twenty-fifth year; and the historical sense involves a perception, not only of the pastness of the past, but of its presence; the historical sense compels a man to write not merely with his own generation in his bones, but with a feeling that the whole of the literature of Europe from Homer and within it the whole of the literature of his own country has a simultaneous existence and composes a simultaneous order. This historical sense, which is a sense of the timeless as well as of the temporal and of the timeless and of the temporal together, is what makes a writer traditional. And it is at the same time what makes a writer most acutely conscious of his place in time, of his contemporaneity.

No poet, no artist of any art, has his complete meaning alone. His significance, his appreciation is the appreciation of his relation to the dead poets and artists. You cannot value him alone; you must set him, for contrast and comparison, among the dead. I mean this as a principle of æsthetic, not merely historical, criticism. The necessity that he shall conform, that he shall cohere, is not one-sided; what happens when a new work of art is created is something that happens simultaneously to all the works of art which preceded it. The existing monuments form an ideal order among themselves, which is modified by the introduction of the new (the really new) work of art among them. The existing order is complete before the new work arrives; for order to persist after the supervention of novelty, the *whole* existing order must be, if ever so slightly, altered; and so the relations, proportions, values of each work of art toward the whole are readjusted; and this is conformity between the old and the new. Whoever has approved this idea of order, of the form of European, of English literature, will not find it preposterous that the past should be altered by the present as much as the present is directed by the past. And the poet who is aware of this will be aware of great difficulties and responsibilities.

In a peculiar sense he will be aware also that he must inevitably be judged by the standards of the past. I say judged, not amputated, by them; not judged to be as good as, or worse or better than, the dead; and certainly not judged by the canons of dead critics. It is a judgment, a comparison, in which two things are measured by each other. To conform merely would be for the new work not really to conform at all; it would not be new, and would therefore not be a work of art. And we do not quite say that the new is more valuable because it fits in; but its fitting in is a test of its value—a test, it is true, which can only be slowly and cautiously applied, for we are none of us infallible judges of conformity. We say: it appears to conform, and is perhaps individual, or it appears individual, and may conform; but we are hardly likely to find that it is one and not the other.

To proceed to a more intelligible exposition of the relation of the poet to the past: he can neither take the past as a lump, an indiscriminate bolus, nor can he form himself wholly on one or two private admirations, nor can he form himself wholly upon one preferred period. The first course is inadmissible, the second is an important experience of youth, and the third is a pleasant and highly desirable supplement. The poet must be very conscious of the main current, which does not at all flow invariably through the most distinguished reputations. He must be quite aware of the obvious fact that art never improves, but that the material of art is never quite the same. He must be aware that the mind of Europe—the mind of his own country—a mind which he learns in time to be much more important than his own private mind—is a mind which changes, and that this change is a development which abandons nothing *en route*, which does not superannuate either Shakespeare, or Homer, or the rock drawing of the Magdalenian draughtsmen. That this development, refinement perhaps, complication certainly, is not, from the point of view of the artist, any improvement. Perhaps not even an improvement from the point of view of the psychologist or not to the extent which we imagine; perhaps only in the end based upon a complication in economics and machinery. But the difference between the present and the past is that the conscious present is an awareness of the past in a way and to an extent which the past's awareness of itself cannot show.

Some one said: "The dead writers are remote from us because we *know* so much more than they did." Precisely, and they are that which we know.

I am alive to a usual objection to what is clearly part of my programme for the *métier* of poetry. The objection is that the doctrine requires a ridiculous amount of erudition (pedantry), a claim which can be rejected by appeal to the lives of poets in any pantheon. It will even be affirmed that much learning deadens or perverts poetic sensibility. While, however, we persist in believing that a poet ought to know as much as will not encroach upon his necessary receptivity and necessary laziness, it is not desirable to confine knowledge to whatever can be put into a useful shape for examinations, drawing-rooms, or the still more pretentious modes of publicity. Some can absorb knowledge, the more tardy must sweat for it. Shakespeare acquired more essential history from Plutarch than most men could from the whole British Museum. What is to be insisted upon is that the poet must develop or procure the consciousness of the past and that he should continue to develop this consciousness throughout his career.

What happens is a continual surrender of himself as he is at the moment to something which is more valuable. The progress of an artist is a continual self-sacrifice, a continual extinction of personality.

There remains to define this process of depersonalization and its relation to the sense of tradition. It is in this depersonalization that art may be said to approach the condition of science. I shall, therefore, invite you to consider, as a suggestive analogy, the action which takes place when a bit of finely filiated platinum is introduced into a chamber containing oxygen and sulphur dioxide.

## II

Honest criticism and sensitive appreciation is directed not upon the poet but upon the poetry. If we attend to the confused cries of the newspaper critics and the susurrus of popular repetition that follows, we shall hear the names of poets in great numbers; if we seek not Blue-book knowledge but the enjoyment of poetry, and ask for a poem, we shall seldom find it. In the last article I tried to point out the importance of the relation of the poem to other poems by other authors, and suggested the conception of poetry as a living whole of all the poetry that has ever been written. The other aspect of this Impersonal theory of poetry is the relation of the poem to its author. And I hinted, by an analogy, that the mind of the mature poet differs from that of the immature one not precisely in any valuation of "personality," not being necessarily more interesting, or having "more to say," but rather by being a more finely perfected medium in which special, or very varied, feelings are at liberty to enter into new combinations.

The analogy was that of the catalyst. When the two gases previously mentioned are mixed in the presence of a filament of platinum, they form sulphurous acid. This combination takes place only if the platinum is present; nevertheless the newly formed acid contains no trace of platinum, and the platinum itself is apparently unaffected; has remained inert, neutral, and unchanged. The mind of the poet is the shred of platinum.

It may partly or exclusively operate upon the experience of the man himself; but, the more perfect the artist, the more completely separate in him will be the man who suffers and the mind which creates; the more perfectly will the mind digest and transmute the passions which are its material.

The experience, you will notice, the elements which enter the presence of the transforming catalyst, are of two kinds: emotions and feelings. The effect of a work of art upon the person who enjoys it is an experience different in kind from any experience not of art. It may be formed out of one emotion, or may be a combination of several; and various feelings, inhering for the writer in particular words or phrases or images, may be added to compose the final result. Or great poetry may be made without the direct use of any emotion whatever: composed out of feelings solely. Canto XV of the *Inferno* (Brunetto Latini) is a working up of the emotion evident in the situation; but the effect, though single as that of any work of art, is obtained by considerable complexity of detail. The last quatrain gives an image, a feeling attaching to an image, which "came," which did not develop simply out of what precedes, but which was probably in suspension in the poet's mind until the proper combination arrived for it to add itself to. The poet's mind is in fact a receptacle for seizing and storing up numberless feelings, phrases, images, which remain there until all the particles which can unite to form a new compound are present together.

If you compare several representative passages of the greatest poetry you see how great is the variety of types of combination, and also how completely any semi-ethical criterion of "sublimity" misses the mark. For it is not the "greatness," the intensity, of the emotions, the components, but the intensity of the artistic process, the pressure, so to speak, under which the fusion takes place, that counts. The episode of Paolo and Francesca employs a definite emotion, but the intensity of the poetry is something quite different from whatever intensity in the supposed experience it may give the impression of. It is no more intense, furthermore, than Canto XXVI, the voyage of Ulysses, which has not the direct dependence upon an emotion. Great variety is possible in the process of transmution of emotion: the murder of Agamemnon, or the agony of Othello, gives an artistic effect apparently closer to a possible original than the scenes from Dante. In the *Agamemnon*, the artistic emotion approximates to the emotion of an actual spectator; in *Othello* to the emotion of the protagonist himself. But the difference between art and the event is always absolute; the combination which is the murder of Agamemnon is probably as complex as that which is the voyage of Ulysses. In either case there has been a fusion of elements. The ode of Keats contains a number of feelings which have nothing particular to do with the nightingale, but which the nightingale, partly, perhaps, because of its attractive name, and partly because of its reputation, served to bring together.

The point of view which I am struggling to attack is perhaps related to the metaphysical theory of the substantial unity of the soul: for my meaning is, that the poet has, not a "personality" to express, but a particular medium, which is only a medium and not a personality, in which impressions and experiences combine in peculiar and unexpected ways. Impressions and experiences which are important for the man may take no place in the poetry, and those which become important in the poetry may play quite a negligible part in the man, the personality.

I will quote a passage which is unfamiliar enough to be regarded with fresh attention in the light—or darkness—of these observations:

> And now methinks I could e'en chide myself
> For doating on her beauty, though her death
> Shall be revenged after no common action.
> Does the silkworm expend her yellow labours
> For thee? For thee does she undo herself?
> Are lordships sold to maintain ladyships
> For the poor benefit of a bewildering minute?
> Why does yon fellow falsify highways,
> And put his life between the judge's lips,
> To refine such a thing—keeps horse and men
> To beat their valours for her? . . .

In this passage (as is evident if it is taken in its context) there is a combination of positive and negative emotions: an intensely strong attraction toward beauty and an equally intense fascination by the ugliness which is contrasted with it and which destroys it. This balance of contrasted emotion is in the dramatic situation to which the speech is pertinent, but that situation alone is inadequate to it. This is, so to speak, the structural emotion, provided by the drama. But the whole effect, the dominant tone, is due to the fact that a number of floating feelings, having an affinity to this emotion by no means superficially evident, have combined with it to give us a new art emotion.

It is not in his personal emotions, the emotions provoked by particular events in his life, that the poet is in any way remarkable or interesting. His particular emotions may be simple, or crude, or flat. The emotion in his poetry will be a very complex thing, but not with the complexity of the emotions of people who have very complex or unusual emotions in life. One error, in fact, of eccentricity in poetry is to seek for new human emotions to express: and in this search for novelty in the wrong place it discovers the perverse. The business of the poet is not to find new emotions, but to use the ordinary ones and, in working them up into poetry, to express feelings which are not in actual emotions at all. And emotions which he has never experienced will serve his turn as well as those familiar to him. Consequently, we must believe that "emotion recollected in tranquillity" is an inexact formula. For it is neither emotion, nor recollection, nor, without distortion of meaning, tranquillity. It is a concentration, and a new thing resulting from the concentration, of a very great number of experiences which to the practical and active person would not seem to be experiences at all; it is a concentration which does not happen consciously or of deliberation. These experiences are not "recollected," and they finally unite in an atmosphere which is "tranquil" only in that it is a passive attending upon the event. Of course this is not quite the whole story. There is a great deal, in the writing of poetry, which must be conscious and deliberate. In fact, the bad poet is usually unconscious where he ought to be conscious, and conscious where he ought to be unconscious. Both errors tend to make him "personal." Poetry is not a turning loose of emotion, but an escape from emotion; it is not the expression of personality, but an escape from personality. But, of course, only those who have personality and emotions know what it means to want to escape from these things.

### III

*ὁ δὲ νοῦς ἴσως θειότερόν τι καὶ ἀπαθές ἐστιν*

This essay proposes to halt at the frontier of metaphysics or mysticism, and confine itself to such practical conclusions as can be applied by the responsible person interested in poetry. To divert interest from the poet to the poetry is a laudable aim: for it would conduce to a juster estimation of actual poetry, good and bad. There are many people who appreciate the expression of sincere emotion in verse, and there is a smaller number of people who can appreciate technical excellence. But very few know when there is expression of *significant* emotion, emotion which has its life in the poem and not in the history of the poet. The emotion of art is impersonal. And the poet cannot reach this impersonality without surrendering himself wholly to the work to be done. And he is not likely to know what is to be done unless he lives in what is not merely the present, but the present moment of the past, unless he is conscious, not of what is dead, but of what is already living.

# THE POSSIBILITY OF A POETIC DRAMA

THE questions—why there is no poetic drama to-day, how the stage has lost all hold on literary art, why so many poetic plays are written which can only be read, and read, if at all, without pleasure—have become insipid, almost academic. The usual conclusion is either that "conditions" are too much for us, or that we really prefer other types of literature, or simply that we are uninspired. As for the last alternative, it is not to be entertained; as for the second, what type do we prefer?; and as for the first, no one has ever shown me "conditions," except of the most superficial. The reasons for raising the question again are first that the majority, perhaps, certainly a large number, of poets hanker for the stage; and second, that a not negligible public appears to want verse plays. Surely there is some legitimate craving, not restricted to a few persons, which only the verse play can satisfy. And surely the critical attitude is to attempt to analyse the conditions and the other data. If there comes to light some conclusive obstacle, the investigation should at least help us to turn our thoughts to more profitable pursuits; and if there is not, we may hope to arrive eventually at some statement of conditions which might be altered. Possibly we shall find that our incapacity has a deeper source: the arts have at times flourished when there was no drama; possibly we are incompetent altogether; in that case the stage will be, not the seat, but at all events a symptom, of the malady.

From the point of view of literature, the drama is only one among several poetic forms. The epic, the ballad, the chanson de geste, the forms of Provence and of Tuscany, all found their perfection by serving particular societies. The forms of Ovid, Catullus, Propertius, served a society different, and in some respects more civilized, than any of these; and in the society of Ovid the drama as a form of art was comparatively insignificant. Nevertheless, the drama is perhaps the most permanent, is capable of greater variation and of expressing more varied types of society, than any other. It varied considerably in England alone; but when one day it was discovered lifeless, subsequent forms which had enjoyed a transitory

34

life were dead too. I am not prepared to undertake the historical survey; but I should say that the poetic drama's autopsy was performed as much by Charles Lamb as by anyone else. For a form is not wholly dead until it is known to be; and Lamb, by exhuming the remains of dramatic life at its fullest, brought a consciousness of the immense gap between present and past. It was impossible to believe, after that, in a dramatic "tradition." The relation of Byron's *English Bards* and the poems of Crabbe to the work of Pope was a continuous tradition; but the relation of *The Cenci* to the great English drama is almost that of a reconstruction to an original. By losing tradition, we lose our hold on the present; but so far as there was any dramatic tradition in Shelley's day there was nothing worth the keeping. There is all the difference between preservation and restoration.

The Elizabethan Age in England was able to absorb a great quantity of new thoughts and new images, almost dispensing with tradition, because it had this great form of its own which imposed itself on everything that came to it. Consequently, the blank verse of their plays accomplished a subtlety and consciousness, even an intellectual power, that no blank verse since has developed or even repeated; elsewhere this age is crude, pedantic, or loutish in comparison with its contemporary France or Italy. The nineteenth century had a good many fresh impressions; but it had no form in which to confine them. Two men, Wordsworth and Browning, hammered out forms for themselves—personal forms, *The Excursion, Sordello, The Ring and the Book, Dramatic Monologues;* but no man can invent a form, create a taste for it, and perfect it too. Tennyson, who might unquestionably have been a consummate master of minor forms, took to turning out large patterns on a machine. As for Keats and Shelley, they were too young to be judged, and they were trying one form after another.

These poets were certainly obliged to consume vast energy in this pursuit of form, which could never lead to a wholly satisfying result. There has only been one Dante; and, after all, Dante had the benefit of years of practice in forms employed and altered by numbers of contemporaries and predecessors; he did not waste the years of youth in metric invention; and when he came to the *Commedia* he knew how to pillage right and left. To have, given into one's hands, a crude form, capable of indefinite refinement, and to be the person to see the possibilities—Shakespeare was very fortunate. And it is perhaps the craving for some such *donnée* which draws us on toward the present mirage of poetic drama.

But it is now very questionable whether there are more than two or three in the present generation who are *capable,* the least little bit, of benefiting by such advantages were they given. At most two or three actu-

ally devote themselves to this pursuit of form for which they have little
or no public recognition. To create a form is not merely to invent a shape,
a rhyme or rhythm. It is also the realization of the whole appropriate content of this rhyme or rhythm. The sonnet of Shakespeare is not merely
such and such a pattern, but a precise way of thinking and feeling. The
*framework* which was provided for the Elizabethan dramatist was not
merely blank verse and the five-act play and the Elizabethan playhouse;
it was not merely the plot—for the poets incorporated, remodelled,
adapted or invented, as occasion suggested. It was also the half-formed
᾽ ὕλη, the "temper of the age" (an unsatisfactory phrase), a preparedness, a
habit on the part of the public, to respond to particular stimuli. There is
a book to be written on the commonplaces of any great dramatic period,
the handling of Fate or Death, the recurrence of mood, tone, situation.
We should see then just how *little* each poet had to do; only so much as
would make a play his, only what was really essential to make it different
from anyone else's. When there is this economy of effort it is possible to
have several, even many, good poets at once. The great ages did not perhaps *produce* much more talent than ours; but less talent was wasted.

Now in a formless age there is very little hope for the minor poet to do
anything worth doing; and when I say minor I mean very good poets
indeed: such as filled the Greek anthology and the Elizabethan song-
books; even a Herrick; but not merely second-rate poets, for Denham and
Waller have quite another importance, occupying points in the development of a major form. When everything is set out for the minor poet to
do, he may quite frequently come upon some *trouvaille,* even in the drama:
Peele and Brome are examples. Under the present conditions, the minor
poet has too much to do. And this leads to another reason for the incom-
petence of our time in poetic drama.

Permanent literature is always a presentation: either a presentation of
thought, or a presentation of feeling by a statement of events in human
action or objects in the external world. In earlier literature—to avoid the
word "classic"—we find both kinds, and sometimes, as in some of the dialogues of Plato, exquisite combinations of both. Aristotle presents
thought, stripped to the essential structure, and he is a great *writer.* The
*Agamemnon* or *Macbeth* is equally a statement, but of events. They are as
much works of the "intellect" as the writings of Aristotle. There are more
recent works of art which have the same quality of intellect in common
with those of Æschylus and Shakespeare and Aristotle: *Education
Sentimentale* is one of them. Compare it with such a book as *Vanity Fair* and
you will see that the labour of the intellect consisted largely in a purifi-
cation, in keeping out a great deal that Thackeray allowed to remain in;

in refraining from reflection, in putting into the statement enough to make reflection unnecessary. The case of Plato is still more illuminating. Take the *Theætetus*. In a few opening words Plato gives a scene, a personality, a feeling, which colour the subsequent discourse but do not interfere with it: the particular setting, and the abstruse theory of knowledge afterwards developed, co-operate without confusion. Could any contemporary author exhibit such control?

In the nineteenth century another mentality manifested itself. It is evident in a very able and brilliant poem, Goethe's *Faust*. Marlowe's Mephistopheles is a simpler creature than Goethe's. But at least Marlowe has, in a few words, concentrated him into a statement. He is there, and (incidentally) he renders Milton's Satan superfluous. Goethe's demon inevitably sends us back to Goethe. He embodies a philosophy. A creation of art should not do that: he should *replace* the philosophy. Goethe has not, that is to say, sacrificed or consecrated his thought to make the drama; the drama is still a means. And this type of mixed art has been repeated by men incomparably smaller than Goethe. We have had one other remarkable work of this type: *Peer Gynt*. And we have had the plays of M. Maeterlinck and M. Claudel.[1]

In the work of Maeterlinck and Claudel on the one hand, and those of M. Bergson on the other, we have the mixture of the genres in which our age delights. Every work of imagination must have a philosophy; and every philosophy must be a work of art—how often have we heard that M. Bergson is an artist! It is a boast of his disciples. It is what the word "art" means to them that is the disputable point. Certain works of philosophy can be called works of art: much of Aristotle and Plato, Spinoza, parts of Hume, Mr. Bradley's *Principles of Logic*, Mr. Russell's essay on "Denoting": clear and beautifully formed thought. But this is not what the admirers of Bergson, Claudel, or Maeterlinck (the philosophy of the latter is a little out of date) mean. They mean precisely what is not clear, but what is an emotional stimulus. And as a mixture of thought and of vision provides more stimulus, by suggesting both, both clear thinking and clear statement of particular objects must disappear.

The undigested "idea" or philosophy, the idea-emotion, is to be found also in poetic dramas which are conscientious attempts to adapt a true structure, Athenian or Elizabethan, to contemporary feeling. It appears sometimes as the attempt to supply the defect of structure by an internal

---

[1] I should except *The Dynasts*. This gigantic panorama is hardly to be called a success, but it is essentially an attempt to present a vision, and "sacrifices" the philosophy to the vision, as all great dramas do. Mr. Hardy has apprehended his matter as a poet and an artist.

structure. "But most important of all is the structure of the incidents. For
Tragedy is an imitation, not of men, but of an action and of life, and life
consists in action, and its end is a mode of action, not a quality."[1]

We have on the one hand the "poetic" drama, imitation Greek, imitation Elizabethan, or modern-philosophical, on the other the comedy of
"ideas," from Shaw to Galsworthy, down to the ordinary social comedy.
The most ramshackle Guitry farce has some paltry idea or comment
upon life put into the mouth of one of the characters at the end. It is said
that the stage can be used for a variety of purposes, that in only one of
them perhaps is it united with literary art. A mute theatre is a possibility
(I do not mean the cinema); the ballet is an actuality (though under-
nourished); opera is an institution; but where you have "imitations of life"
on the stage, with speech, the only standard that we can allow is the standard of the work of art, aiming at the same intensity at which poetry and
the other forms of art aim. From that point of view the Shavian drama is
a hybrid as the Maeterlinckian drama is, and we need express no surprise
at their belonging to the same epoch. Both philosophies are populariza-
tions: the moment an idea has been transferred from its pure state in
order that it may become comprehensible to the inferior intelligence it
has lost contact with art. It can remain pure only by being stated simply
in the form of general truth, or by being transmuted, as the attitude of
Flaubert toward the small bourgeois is transformed in *Education
Sentimentale*. It has there become so identified with the reality that you
can no longer say what the idea is.

The essential is not, of course, that drama should be written in verse,
or that we should be able to extenuate our appreciation of broad farce by
occasionally attending a performance of a play of Euripides where
Professor Murray's translation is sold at the door. The essential is to get
upon the stage this precise statement of life which is at the same time a
point of view, a world—a world which the author's mind has subjected to
a complete process of simplification. I do not find that any drama which
"embodies a philosophy" of the author's (like *Faust*) or which illustrates
any social theory (like Shaw's) can possibly fulfil the requirements—
though a place might be left for Shaw if not for Goethe. And the world of
Ibsen and the world of Tchehov are not enough simplified, universal.

Finally, we must take into account the instability of any art—the
drama, music, dancing—which depends upon representation by performers. The intervention of performers introduces a complication of
economic conditions which is in itself likely to be injurious. A struggle,

[1] *Poetics*, vi. 9. Butcher's translation.

more or less unconscious, between the creator and the interpreter is almost inevitable. The interest of a performer is almost certain to be centred in himself: a very slight acquaintance with actors and musicians will testify. The performer is interested not in form but in opportunities for virtuosity or in the communication of his "personality"; the formlessness, the lack of intellectual clarity and distinction in modern music, the great physical stamina and physical training which it often requires, are perhaps signs of the triumph of the performer. The consummation of the triumph of the actor over the play is perhaps the productions of the Guitry.

The conflict is one which certainly cannot be terminated by the utter rout of the actor profession. For one thing, the stage appeals to too many demands besides the demand for art for that to be possible; and also we need, unfortunately, something more than refined automatons. Occasionally attempts have been made to "get around" the actor, to envelop him in masks, to set up a few "conventions" for him to stumble over, or even to develop little breeds of actors for some special Art drama. This meddling with nature seldom succeeds; nature usually overcomes these obstacles. Possibly the majority of attempts to confect a poetic drama have begun at the wrong end; they have aimed at the small public which wants "poetry." ("Novices," says Aristotle, "in the art attain to finish of diction and precision of portraiture before they can construct the plot.") The Elizabethan drama was aimed at a public which wanted *entertainment* of a crude sort, but would *stand* a good deal of poetry; our problem should be to take a form of entertainment, and subject it to the process which would leave it a form of art. Perhaps the music-hall comedian is the best material. I am aware that this is a dangerous suggestion to make. For every person who is likely to consider it seriously there are a dozen toymakers who would leap to tickle æsthetic society into one more quiver and giggle of art debauch. Very few treat art seriously. There are those who treat it solemnly, and will continue to write poetic pastiches of Euripides and Shakespeare; and there are others who treat it as a joke.

# EURIPIDES AND PROFESSOR MURRAY

THE recent appearance of Miss Sybil Thorndyke as Medea at the Holborn Empire is an event which has a bearing upon three subjects of considerable interest: the drama, the present standing of Greek literature, and the importance of good contemporary translation. On the occasion on which I was present the performance was certainly a success; the audience was large, it was attentive, and its applause was long. Whether the success was due to Euripides is uncertain; whether it was due to Professor Murray is not proved; but that it was in considerable measure due to Miss Thorndyke there is no doubt. To have held the centre of the stage for two hours in a rôle which requires both extreme violence and restraint, a rôle which requires simple force and subtle variation; to have sustained such a rôle almost without support; this was a legitimate success. The audience, or what could be seen of it from one of the cheaper seats, was serious and respectful and perhaps inclined to self-approval at having attended the performance of a Greek play; but Miss Thorndyke's acting might have held almost any audience. It employed all the conventions, the theatricalities, of the modern stage; yet her personality triumphed over not only Professor Murray's verse but her own training.

The question remains whether the production was a "work of art." The rest of the cast appeared slightly ill at ease; the nurse was quite a tolerable nurse of the crone type; Jason was negative; the messenger was uncomfortable at having to make such a long speech; and the refined Dalcroze chorus had mellifluous voices which rendered their lyrics happily inaudible. All this contributed toward the high-brow effect which is so depressing; and we imagine that the actors of Athens, who had to speak clearly enough for 20,000 auditors to be able to criticize the versification, would have been pelted with figs and olives had they mumbled so unintelligibly as most of this troupe. But the Greek actor spoke in his own language, and our actors were forced to speak in the language of Professor Gilbert Murray. So that on the whole we may say that the performance was an interesting one.

I do not believe, however, that such performances will do very much to rehabilitate Greek literature or our own, unless they stimulate a desire for better translations. The serious auditors, many of whom I observed to be like myself provided with Professor Murray's eighteenpenny translation, were probably not aware that Miss Thorndyke, in order to succeed as well as she did, was really engaged in a struggle against the translator's verse. She triumphed over it by attracting our attention to her expression and tone and making us neglect her words; and this, of course, was not the dramatic method of Greek acting at its best. The English and Greek languages remained where they were. But few persons realize that the Greek language and the Latin language, and, *therefore*, we say, the English language, are within our lifetime passing through a critical period. The Classics have, during the latter part of the nineteenth century and up to the present moment, lost their place as a pillar of the social and political system—such as the Established Church still is. If they are to survive, to justify themselves as literature, as an element in the European mind, as the foundation for the literature we hope to create, they are very badly in need of persons capable of expounding them. We need some one—not a member of the Church of Rome, and perhaps preferably not a member of the Church of England—to explain how vital a matter it is, if Aristotle may be said to have been a moral pilot of Europe, whether we shall or shall not drop that pilot. And we need a number of educated poets who shall at least have opinions about Greek drama, and whether it is or is not of any use to us. And it must be said that Professor Gilbert Murray is not the man for this. Greek poetry will never have the slightest vitalizing effect upon English poetry if it can only appear masquerading as a vulgar debasement of the eminently personal idiom of Swinburne. These are strong words to use against the most popular Hellenist of his time; but we must witness of Professor Murray ere we die that these things are not otherwise but thus.

This is really a point of capital importance. That the most conspicuous Greek propagandist of the day should almost habitually use two words where the Greek language requires one, and where the English language will provide him with one; that he should render σκιάν by "*grey* shadow"; and that he should stretch the Greek brevity to fit the loose frame of William Morris, and blur the Greek lyric to the fluid haze of Swinburne; these are not faults of infinitesimal insignificance. The first great speech of Medea Mr. Murray begins with:

Women of Corinth, I am come to show
My face, lest ye despise me. . . .

We find in the Greek, ἐξῆλθον δόμων. "Show my face," therefore, is Mr. Murray's gift.

> This thing undreamed of, sudden from on high,
> Hath sapped my soul: I dazzle where I stand,
> The cup of all life shattered in my hand. . . .

Again, we find that the Greek is:

> ἐμοὶ δ' ἄελπτον πρᾶγμα προσπεσὸν τόδε
> ψυχὴν διέφθαρκ'· οἴχομαι δὲ καὶ βίου
> χάριν μεθεῖσα κατθανεῖν χρῄζω, φίλαι.

So, here are two striking phrases which we owe to Mr. Murray; it is he who has sapped our soul and shattered the cup of all life for Euripides. And these are only random examples.

> οὐκ ἔστιν ἄλλη φρὴν μιαιφονωτέρα

becomes "no bloodier spirit between heaven and hell"! Surely we know that Professor Murray is acquainted with "Sister Helen?" Professor Murray has simply interposed between Euripides and ourselves a barrier more impenetrable than the Greek language. We do not reproach him or preferring, apparently, Euripides to Æschylus. But if he does, he should at least appreciate Euripides. And it is inconceivable that anyone with a genuine feeling for the sound of Greek verse should deliberately elect the William Morris couplet, the Swinburne lyric, as a just equivalent.

As a poet, Mr. Murray is merely a very insignificant follower of the pre-Raphaelite movement. As a Hellenist, he is very much of the present day, and a very important figure in the day. This day began, in a sense, with Tylor and a few German anthropologists; since then we have acquired sociology and social psychology, we have watched the clinics of Ribot and Janet, we have read books from Vienna and heard a discourse of Bergson; a philosophy arose at Cambridge; social emancipation crawled abroad; our historical knowledge has of course increased; and we have a curious Freudian-social-mystical-rationalistic-higher-critical interpretation of the Classics and what used to be called the Scriptures. I do not deny the very great value of all work by scientists in their own departments, the great interest also of this work in detail and in its consequences. Few books are more fascinating than those of Miss Harrison, Mr. Cornford, or Mr. Cooke, when they burrow in the origins of Greek myths and rites; M. Durkheim, with his social consciousness, and M.

Levy-Bruhl, with his Bororo Indians who convince themselves that they are parroquets, are delightful writers. A number of sciences have sprung up in an almost tropical exuberance which undoubtedly excites our admiration, and the garden, not unnaturally, has come to resemble a jungle. Such men as Tylor, and Robertson Smith, and Wilhelm Wundt, who early fertilized the soil, would hardly recognize the resulting vegetation; and indeed poor Wundt's *Völkerpsychologie* was a musty relic before it was translated.

All these events are useful and important in their phase, and they have sensibly affected our attitude towards the Classics; and it is this phase of classical study that Professor Murray—the friend and inspirer of Miss Jane Harrison—represents. The Greek is no longer the awe-inspiring Belvedere of Winckelmann, Goethe, and Schopenhauer, the figure of which Walter Pater and Oscar Wilde offered us a slightly debased re-edition. And we realize better how different—not how much more Olympian—were the conditions of the Greek civilization from ours; and at the same time Mr. Zimmern has shown us how the Greek dealt with analogous problems. Incidentally we do not believe that a good English prose style can be modelled upon Cicero, or Tacitus, or Thucydides. If Pindar bores us, we admit it; we are not certain that Sappho was *very* much greater than Catullus; we hold various opinions about Vergil; and we think more highly of Petronius than our grandfathers did.

It is to be hoped that we may be grateful to Professor Murray and his friends for what they have done, while we endeavour to neutralize Professor Murray's influence upon Greek literature and English language in his translations by making better translations. The choruses from Euripides by H. D. are, allowing for errors and even occasional omissions of difficult passages, much nearer to both Greek and English than Mr. Murray's. But H. D. and the other poets of the "Poets' Translation Series" have so far done no more than pick up some of the more romantic crumbs of Greek literature; none of them has yet shown himself competent to attack the *Agamemnon*. If we are to digest the heavy food of historical and scientific knowledge that we have eaten we must be prepared for much greater exertions. We need a digestion which can assimilate both Homer and Flaubert. We need a careful study of Renaissance Humanists and Translators, such as Mr. Pound has begun. We need an eye which can see the past in its place with its definite differences from the present, and yet so lively that it shall be as present to us us the present. This is the creative eye; and it is because Professor Murray has no creative instinct that he leaves Euripides quite dead.

# "RHETORIC" AND POETIC DRAMA

THE death of Rostand is the disappearance of the poet whom, more than any other in France, we treated as the exponent of "rhetoric," thinking of rhetoric as something recently out of fashion. And as we find ourselves looking back rather tenderly upon the author of *Cyrano* we wonder what this vice or quality is that is associated as plainly with Rostand's merits as with his defects. His rhetoric, at least, suited him at times so well, and so much better than it suited a much greater poet, Baudelaire, who is at times as rhetorical as Rostand. And we begin to suspect that the word is merely a vague term of abuse for any style that is bad, that is so evidently bad or second-rate that we do not recognize the necessity for greater precision in the phrases we apply to it.

Our own Elizabethan and Jacobean poetry—in so nice a problem it is much safer to stick to one's own language—is repeatedly called "rhetorical." It had this and that notable quality, but, when we wish to admit that it had defects, it is rhetorical. It had serious defects, even gross faults, but we cannot be considered to have erased them from our language when we are so unclear in our perception of what they are. The fact is that both Elizabethan prose and Elizabethan poetry are written in a variety of styles with a variety of vices. Is the style of Lyly, is Euphuism, rhetorical? In contrast to the elder style of Ascham and Elyot which it assaults, it is a clear, flowing, orderly and relatively pure style, with a systematic if monotonous formula of antitheses and similes. Is the style of Nashe? A tumid, flatulent, vigorous style very different from Lyly's. Or it is perhaps the strained and the mixed figures of speech in which Shakespeare indulged himself. Or it is perhaps the careful declamation of Jonson. The word simply cannot be used as synonymous with bad writing. The meanings which it has been obliged to shoulder have been mostly opprobrious; but if a precise meaning can be found for it this meaning may occasionally represent a virtue. It is one of those words which it is the business of criticism to dissect and reassemble. Let us avoid the assumption that rhetoric is a vice of manner, and endeavour to find a rhetoric of substance also, which is right because it issues from what it has to express.

At the present time there is a manifest preference for the "conversational" in poetry—the style of "direct speech," opposed to the "oratorical" and the rhetorical; but if rhetoric is any convention of writing inappropriately applied, this conversational style can and does become a rhetoric—or what is supposed to be a conversational style, for it is often as remote from polite discourse as well could be. Much of the second and third rate in American *vers libre* is of this sort; and much of the second and third rate in English Wordsworthianism. There is in fact no conversational or other form which can be applied indiscriminately; if a writer wishes to give the effect of speech he must positively give the effect of himself talking in his own person or in one of his rôles; and if we are to express ourselves, our variety of thoughts and feelings, on a variety of subjects with inevitable rightness, we must adapt our manner to the moment with infinite variations. Examination of the development of Elizabethan drama shows this progress in adaptation, a development from monotony to variety, a progressive refinement in the perception of the variations of feeling, and a progressive elaboration of the means of expressing these variations. This drama is admitted to have grown away from the rhetorical expression, the bombast speeches, of Kyd and Marlowe to the subtle and dispersed utterance of Shakespeare and Webster. But this apparent abandonment or outgrowth of rhetoric is two things: it is partly an improvement in language and it is partly progressive variation in feeling. There is, of course, a long distance separating the furibund fluency of old Hieronimo and the broken words of Lear. There is also a difference between the famous

> Oh eyes no eyes, but fountains full of tears!
> Oh life no life, but lively form of death!

and the superb "additions to Hieronimo."[1]

We think of Shakespeare perhaps as the dramatist who concentrates everything into a sentence, "Pray you undo this button," or "Honest honest Iago"; we forget that there is a rhetoric proper to Shakespeare at his best period which is quite free from the genuine Shakespearean vices

---

[1] Of the authorship it can only be said that the lines are by some admirer of Marlowe. This might well be Jonson.

either of the early period or the late. These passages are comparable to the best bombast of Kyd or Marlowe, with a greater command of language and a greater control of the emotion. *The Spanish Tragedy* is bombastic when it descends to language which was only the trick of its age; *Tamburlaine* is bombastic because it is monotonous, inflexible to the alterations of emotion. The really fine rhetoric of Shakespeare occurs in situations where a character in the play *sees himself* in a dramatic light:

> *Othello.*      And say, besides,—that in Aleppo once . . .
>
> *Coriolanus.*  If you have writ your annals true, 'tis there,
>                That like an eagle in a dovecote, I
>                Fluttered your Volscians in Corioli.
>                Alone I did it.   Boy!
>
> *Timon.*       Come not to me again; but say to Athens,
>                Timon hath made his everlasting mansion
>                Upon the beachèd verge of the salt flood . . .

It occurs also once in *Antony and Cleopatra*, when Enobarbus is inspired to see Cleopatra in this dramatic light:

> The barge she sat in . . .

Shakespeare made fun of Marston, and Jonson made fun of Kyd. But in Monston's play the words were expressive of nothing; and Jonson was criticizing the feeble and conceited language, not the emotion, not the "oratory." Jonson is as oratorical himself, and the moments when his oratory succeeds are, I believe, the moments that conform to our formula. Notably the speech of Sylla's ghost in the induction to *Catiline*, and the speech of Envy at the beginning of *The Poetaster*. These two figures are contemplating their own dramatic importance, and quite properly. But in the Senate speeches in *Catiline*, how tedious, how dusty! Here we are spectators not of a play of characters, but of a play of forensic, exactly as if we had been forced to attend the sitting itself. A speech in a play should never appear to be intended to move us as it might conceivably move other characters in the play, for it is essential that we should preserve our position of spectators, and observe always from the outside though with complete understanding. The scene in *Julius Cæsar* is right because the object of our attention is not the speech of Antony *(Bedeutung)* but the effect of his speech upon the mob, and Antony's intention, his preparation and consciousness of the effect. And in the rhetorical speeches from

Shakespeare which have been cited, we have this necessary advantage of a new clue to the character, in noting the angle from which he views himself. But when a character *in* a play makes a direct appeal to us, we are either the victims of our own sentiment, or we are in the presence of a vicious rhetoric.

These references ought to supply some evidence of the propriety of Cyrano on Noses. Is not Cyrano exactly in this position of contemplating himself as a romantic, a dramatic figure? This dramatic sense on the part of the characters themselves is rare in modern drama. In sentimental drama it appears in a degraded form, when we are evidently intended to accept the character's sentimental interpretation of himself. In plays of realism we often find parts which are never allowed to be consciously dramatic, for fear, perhaps, of their appearing less real. But in actual life, in many of those situations in actual life which we enjoy consciously and keenly, we are at times aware of ourselves in this way, and these moments are of very great usefulness to dramatic verse. A very small part of acting is that which takes place on the stage! Rostand had—whether he had anything else or not—this dramatic sense, and it is what gives life to Cyrano. It is a sense which is almost a sense of humour (for when anyone is conscious of himself as acting, something like a sense of humour is present). It gives Rostand's characters—Cyrano at least—a gusto which is uncommon on the modern stage. No doubt Rostand's people play up to this too steadily. We recognize that in the love scenes of Cyrano in the garden, for in *Romeo and Juliet* the profounder dramatist shows his lovers melting into incoherent unconsciousness of their isolated selves, shows the human soul in the process of forgetting itself. Rostand could not do that; but in the particular case of Cyrano on Noses, the character, the situation, the occasion were perfectly suited and combined. The tirade generated by this combination is not only genuinely and highly dramatic: it is possibly poetry also. If a writer is incapable of composing such a scene as this, so much the worse for his poetic drama.

*Cyrano* satisfies, as far as scenes like this can satisfy, the requirements of poetic drama. It must take genuine and substantial human emotions, such emotions as observation can confirm, typical emotions, and give them artistic form; the degree of abstraction is a question for the method of each author. In Shakespeare the form is determined in the unity of the whole, as well as single scenes; it is something to attain this unity, as Rostand does, in scenes if not the whole play. Not only as a dramatist, but as a poet, he is superior to Maeterlinck, whose drama, in failing to be dramatic, fails also to be poetic. Maeterlinck has a literary perception of the dramatic and a literary perception of the poetic, and he joins the two; the two are not, as sometimes they are in the work of Rostand, fused. His characters take no conscious delight in their rôle—they are sentimental. With Rostand the centre of gravity is in the expression of the emotion, not as with Maeterlinck in the emotion which cannot be expressed. Some writers appear to believe that emotions gain in intensity through being inarticulate. Perhaps the emotions are not significant enough to endure full daylight.

In any case, we may take our choice: we may apply the term "rhetoric" to the type of dramatic speech which I have instanced, and then we must admit that it covers good as well as bad. Or we may choose to except this type of speech from rhetoric. In that case we must say that rhetoric is any adornment or inflation of speech which is *not done for a particular effect* but for a general impressiveness. And in this case, too, we cannot allow the term to cover all bad writing.

# SOME NOTES ON THE BLANK VERSE
# OF CHRISTOPHER MARLOWE

"Marloe was stabd with a dagger, and dyed swearing"

A MORE friendly critic, Mr. A. C. Swinburne, observes of this poet that "the father of English tragedy and the creator of English blank verse was therefore also the teacher and the guide of Shakespeare." In this sentence there are two misleading assumptions and two misleading conclusions. Kyd has as good a title to the first honour as Marlowe; Surrey has a better title to the second; and Shakespeare was not taught or guided by one of his predecessors or contemporaries alone. The less questionable judgment is, that Marlowe exercised a strong influence over later drama, though not himself as great a dramatist as Kyd; that he introduced several new tones into blank verse, and commenced the dissociative process which drew it farther and farther away from the rhythms of rhymed verse; and that when Shakespeare borrowed from him, which was pretty often at the beginning, Shakespeare either made something inferior or something different.

The comparative study of English versification at various periods is a large tract of unwritten history. To make a study of blank verse alone, would be to elicit some curious conclusions. It would show, I believe, that blank verse within Shakespeare's lifetime was more highly developed, that it became the vehicle of more varied and more intense art-emotions than it has ever conveyed since; and that after the erection of the Chinese Wall of Milton, blank verse has suffered not only arrest but retrogression. That the blank verse of Tennyson, for example, a consummate master of this form in certain applications, is cruder (*not* "rougher" or less perfect in technique) than that of half a dozen contemporaries of Shakespeare; cruder, because less capable of expressing complicated, subtle, and surprising emotions.

Every writer who has written any blank verse worth saving has produced particular tones which his verse and no other's is capable of rendering; and we should keep this in mind when we talk about "influences" and "indebtedness." Shakespeare is "universal" (if you like) because he has

49

more of these tones than anyone else; but they are all out of the one man; one man cannot be more than one man; there might have been six Shakespeares at once without conflicting frontiers; and to say that Shakespeare expressed nearly all human emotions, implying that he left very little for anyone else, is a radical misunderstanding of art and the artist—a misunderstanding which, even when explicitly rejected, may lead to our neglecting the effort of attention necessary to discover the specific properties of the verse of Shakespeare's contemporaries. The development of blank verse may be likened to the analysis of that astonishing industrial product coal-tar. Marlowe's verse is one of the earlier derivatives, but it possesses properties which are not repeated in any of the analytic or synthetic blank verses discovered somewhat later.

The "vices of style" of Marlowe's and Shakespeare's age is a convenient name for a number of vices, no one of which, perhaps, was shared by all of the writers. It is pertinent, at least, to remark that Marlowe's "rhetoric" is not, or not characteristically, Shakespeare's rhetoric; that Marlowe's rhetoric consists in a pretty simple huffe-snuffe bombast, while Shakespeare's is more exactly a vice of style, a tortured perverse ingenuity of images which dissipates instead of concentrating the imagination, and which may be due in part to influences by which Marlowe was untouched. Next, we find that Marlowe's vice is one which he was gradually attenuating, and even, what is more miraculous, turning into a virtue. And we find that this bard of torrential imagination recognized many of his best bits (and those of one or two others), saved them, and reproduced them more than once, almost invariably improving them in the process.

It is worth while noticing a few of these versions, because they indicate, somewhat contrary to usual opinion, that Marlowe was a deliberate and conscious workman. Mr. J. G. Robertson has spotted an interesting theft of Marlowe's from Spenser. Here is Spenser (*Faery Queen*, I. vii. 32):

> Like to an almond tree y-mounted high
>   On top of green Selinis all alone,
> With blossoms brave bedeckèd daintily;
>   Whose tender locks do tremble every one
> At every little breath that under heaven is blown.

And here Marlowe (*Tamburlaine*, Part II. Act IV. sc. iii.):

> Like to an almond tree y-mounted high
> Upon the lofty and celestial mount
> Of evergreen Selinus, quaintly deck'd
> With blooms more white than Erycina's brows,

> Whose tender blossoms tremble every one
> At every little breath that thorough heaven is blown.

This is interesting, not only as showing that Marlowe's talent, like that of most poets, was partly synthetic, but also because it seems to give a clue to some particularly "lyric" effects found in *Tamburlaine*, not in Marlowe's other plays, and not, I believe, anywhere else. For example, the praise of Zenocrate in Part II. Act. II. sc. iv.:

> Now walk the angels on the walls of heaven,
> As sentinels to warn th' immortal souls
> To entertain divine Zenocrate: etc.

This is not Spenser's movement, but the influence of Spenser must be present. There had been no great blank verse before Marlowe; but there was the powerful presence of this great master of melody immediately precedent; and the combination produced results which could not be repeated. I do not think that it can be claimed that Peele had any influence here.

The passage quoted from Spenser has a further interest. It will be noted that the fourth line:

> With blooms more white than Erycina's brows

is Marlowe's contribution. Compare this with these other lines of Marlowe:

> So looks my love, shadowing in her brows
> > *(Tamburlaine)*
> Like to the shadows of Pyramides
> > *(Tamburlaine)*

and the final and best version:

> Shadowing more beauty in their airy brows
> Than have the white breasts of the queen of love.
> > *(Doctor Faustus)*

and compare the whole set with Spenser again *(F. Q.)*:

> Upon her eyelids many graces sate
> Under the shadow of her even brows,

a passage which Mr. Robertson says Spenser himself used in three other places.

This economy is frequent in Marlowe. Within *Tamburlaine* it occurs in the form of monotony, especially in the facile use of resonant names (*e.g.* the recurrence of "Caspia" or "Caspian" with the same tone effect), a practice in which Marlowe was followed by Milton, but which Marlowe himself outgrew. Again,

> Zenocrate, lovlier than the love of Jove,
> Brighter than is the silver Rhodope,

is paralleled later by

> Zenocrate, the lovliest maid alive,
> Fairer than rocks of pearl and precious stone.

One line Marlowe remodels with triumphant success:

> And set black streamers in the firmament
> *(Tamburlaine)*

becomes

> See, see, where Christ's blood streams in the firmament!
> *(Doctor Faustus)*

The verse accomplishments of *Tamburlaine* are notably two: Marlowe gets into blank verse the melody of Spenser, and he gets a new driving power by reinforcing the sentence period against the line period. The rapid long sentence, running line into line, as in the famous soliloquies "Nature compounded of four elements" and "What is beauty, saith my sufferings, then?" marks the certain escape of blank verse from the rhymed couplet, and from the elegiac or rather pastoral note of Surrey, to which Tennyson returned. If you contrast these two soliloquies with the verse of Marlowe's greatest contemporary, Kyd—by no means a despicable versifier—you see the importance of the innovation:

> The one took sanctuary, and, being sent for out,
> Was murdered in Southwark as he passed
> To Greenwich, where the Lord Protector lay.
> Black Will was burned in Flushing on a stage;
> Green was hanged at Osbridge in Kent . . .

which is not really inferior to:

> So these four abode
> Within one house together; and as years
> Went forward, Mary took another mate;
> But Dora lived unmarried till her death.
>
> (Tennyson, *Dora*)

In *Faustus* Marlowe went farther: he broke up the line, to a gain in intensity, in the last soliloquy; and he developed a new and important conversational tone in the dialogues of Faustus with the devil. *Edward II.* has never lacked consideration: it is more desirable, in brief space, to remark upon two plays, one of which has been misunderstood and the other underrated. These are the *Jew of Malta* and *Dido Queen of Carthage.* Of the first of these, it has always been said that the end, even the last two acts, are unworthy of the first three. If one takes the *Jew of Malta* not as a tragedy, or as a "tragedy of blood," but as a farce, the concluding act becomes intelligible; and if we attend with a careful ear to the versification, we find that Marlowe develops a tone to suit this farce, and even perhaps that this tone is his most powerful and mature tone. I say farce, but with the enfeebled humour of our times the word is a misnomer; it is the farce of the old English humour, the terribly serious, even savage comic humour, the humour which spent its last breath on the decadent genius of Dickens. It has nothing in common with J. M. Barrie, Captain Bairnsfather, or *Punch*. It is the humour of that very serious (but very different) play, *Volpone*.

> First, be thou void of these affections,
> Compassion, love, vain hope, and heartless fear;
> Be moved at nothing, see thou pity none . . .
> As for myself, I walk abroad o' nights,
> And kill sick people groaning under walls:
> Sometimes I go about and poison wells . . .

and the last words of Barabas complete this prodigious caricature:

> But now begins th' extremity of heat
> To pinch me with intolerable pangs:
> Die, life! fly, soul! tongue, curse thy fill, and die!

It is something which Shakespeare could not do, and which he could not have understood.

*Dido* appears to be a hurried play, perhaps done to order with the *Æneid* in front of him. But even here there is progress. The account of the sack of

Troy is in this newer style of Marlowe's, this style which secures its emphasis by always hesitating on the edge of caricature at the right moment:

> The Grecian soldiers, tir'd with ten years war,
> Began to cry, "Let us unto our ships,
> Troy is invincible, why stay we here?" . . .
>
> But this, the camp was come unto the walls,
> And through the breach did march into the streets,
> Where, meeting with the rest, "Kill, kill!" they cried. . . .
>
> And after him, his band of Myrmidons,
> With balls of wild-fire in their murdering paws . . .
>
> At last, the soldiers pull'd her by the heels,
> And swung her howling in the empty air. . . .
>
> We saw Cassandra sprawling in the streets . . .

This is not Vergil, or Shakespeare; it is pure Marlowe. By comparing the whole speech with Clarence's dream, in *Richard III.*, one acquires a little insight into the difference between Marlowe and Shakespeare:

> What scourge for perjury
> Can this dark monarchy afford false Clarence?

There, on the other hand, is what Marlowe's style could not do; the phrase has a concision which is almost classical, certainly Dantesque. Again, as often with the Elizabethan dramatists, there are lines in Marlowe, besides the many lines that Shakespeare adapted, that might have been written by either:

> If thou wilt stay,
> Leap in mine arms; mine arms are open wide;
> If not, turn from me, and I'll turn from thee;
> For though thou hast the heart to say farewell,
> I have not power to stay thee.

But the direction in which Marlowe's verse might have moved, had he not "dyed swearing," is quite un-Shakespearean, is toward this intense and serious and indubitably great poetry, which, like some great painting and sculpture, attains its effects by something not unlike caricature.

## HAMLET AND HIS PROBLEMS

FEW critics have admitted that *Hamlet* the play is the primary problem, and Hamlet the character only secondary. And Hamlet the character has had an especial temptation for that most dangerous type of critic: the critic with a mind which is naturally of the creative order, but which through some weakness in creative power exercises itself in criticism instead. These minds often find in Hamlet a vicarious existence for their own artistic realization. Such a mind had Goethe, who made of Hamlet a Werther; and such had Coleridge, who made of Hamlet a Coleridge; and probably neither of these men in writing about Hamlet remembered that his first business was to study a work of art. The kind of criticism that Goethe and Coleridge produced, in writing of Hamlet, is the most misleading kind possible. For they both possessed unquestionable critical insight, and both make their critical aberrations the more plausible by the substitution—of their own Hamlet for Shakespeare's—which their creative gift effects. We should be thankful that Walter Pater did not fix his attention on this play.

Two recent writers, Mr. J. M. Robertson and Professor Stoll of the University of Minnesota, have issued small books which can be praised for moving in the other direction. Mr. Stoll performs a service in recalling to our attention the labours of the critics of the seventeenth and eighteenth centuries,[1] observing that

> they knew less about psychology than more recent Hamlet critics, but they were nearer in spirit to Shakespeare's art; and as they insisted on the importance of the effect of the whole rather than on the importance of the leading character, they were nearer, in their old-fashioned way, to the secret of dramatic art in general.

---

[1] I have never, by the way, seen a cogent refutation of Thomas Rymer's objections to *Othello.*

*Qua* work of art, the work of art cannot be interpreted; there is nothing
to interpret; we can only criticize it according to standards, in comparison
to other works of art; and for "interpretation" the chief task is the presentation of relevant historical facts which the reader is not assumed to
know. Mr. Robertson points out, very pertinently, how critics have failed
in their "interpretation" of *Hamlet* by ignoring what ought to be very
obvious: that *Hamlet* is a stratification, that it represents the efforts of a
series of men, each making what he could out of the work of his predecessors. The *Hamlet* of Shakespeare will appear to us very differently if,
instead of treating the whole action of the play as due to Shakespeare's
design, we perceive his *Hamlet* to be superposed upon much cruder material which persists even in the final form.

We know that there was an older play by Thomas Kyd, that extraordinary dramatic (if not poetic) genius who was in all probability the author
of two plays so dissimilar as the *Spanish Tragedy* and *Arden of Feversham;*
and what this play was like we can guess from three clues: from the
*Spanish Tragedy* itself, from the tale of Belleforest upon which Kyd's
*Hamlet* must have been based, and from a version acted in Germany in
Shakespeare's lifetime which bears strong evidence of having been adapted from the earlier, not the later, play. From these three sources it is clear
that in the earlier play the motive was a revenge-motive simply; that the
action or delay is caused, as in the *Spanish Tragedy,* solely by the difficulty of assassinating a monarch surrounded by guards; and that the "madness" of Hamlet was feigned in order to escape suspicion, and successfully. In the final play of Shakespeare, on the other hand, there is a motive
which is more important than that of revenge, and which explicitly
"blunts" the latter; the delay in revenge is unexplained on grounds of
necessity or expediency; and the effect of the "madness" is not to lull but
to arouse the king's suspicion. The alteration is not complete enough,
however, to be convincing. Furthermore, there are verbal parallels so
close to the *Spanish Tragedy* as to leave no doubt that in places Shakespeare
was merely *revising* the text of Kyd. And finally there are unexplained
scenes—the Polonius-Laertes and the Polonius-Reynaldo scenes—for
which there is little excuse; these scenes are not in the verse style of Kyd,
and not beyond doubt in the style of Shakespeare. These Mr. Robertson
believes to be scenes in the original play of Kyd reworked by a third hand,
perhaps Chapman, before Shakespeare touched the play. And he concludes,
with very strong show of reason, that the original play of Kyd was, like
certain other revenge plays, in two parts of five acts each. The upshot of
Mr. Robertson's examination is, we believe, irrefragable: that Shakespeare's
*Hamlet,* so far as it is Shakespeare's, is a play dealing with the effect of a

mother's guilt upon her son, and that Shakespeare was unable to impose this motive successfully upon the "intractable" material of the old play.

Of the intractability there can be no doubt. So far from being Shakespeare's masterpiece, the play is most certainly an artistic failure. In several ways the play is puzzling, and disquieting as is none of the others. Of all the plays it is the longest and is possibly the one on which Shakespeare spent most pains; and yet he has left in it superfluous and inconsistent scenes which even hasty revision should have noticed. The versification is variable. Lines like

> Look, the morn, in russet mantle clad,
> Walks o'er the dew of yon high eastern hill,

are of the Shakespeare of *Romeo and Juliet*. The lines in Act v. sc. ii.,

> Sir, in my heart there was a kind of fighting
> That would not let me sleep . . .
> Up from my cabin,
> My sea-gown scarf'd about me, in the dark
> Grop'd I to find out them: had my desire;
> Finger'd their packet;

are of his quite mature. Both workmanship and thought are in an unstable condition. We are surely justified in attributing the play, with that other profoundly interesting play of "intractable" material and astonishing versification, *Measure for Measure*, to a period of crisis, after which follow the tragic successes which culminate in *Coriolanus*. *Coriolanus* may be not as "interesting" as *Hamlet*, but it is, with *Antony and Cleopatra*, Shakespeare's most assured artistic success. And probably more people have thought *Hamlet* a work of art because they found it interesting, than have found it interesting because it is a work of art. It is the "Mona Lisa" of literature.

The grounds of *Hamlet's* failure are not immediately obvious. Mr. Robertson is undoubtedly correct in concluding that the essential emotion of the play is the feeling of a son towards a guilty mother:

> [Hamlet's] tone is that of one who has suffered tortures on the score of his mother's degradation. . . . The guilt of a mother is an almost intolerable motive for drama, but it had to be maintained and emphasized to supply a psychological solution, or rather a hint of one

This, however, is by no means the whole story. It is not merely the "guilt of a mother" that cannot be handled as Shakespeare handled the suspicion of Othello, the infatuation of Antony, or the pride of Coriolanus. The subject might conceivably have expanded into a tragedy like these, intelligible, self-complete, in the sunlight. *Hamlet,* like the sonnets, is full of some stuff that the writer could not drag to light, contemplate, or manipulate into art. And when we search for this feeling, we find it, as in the sonnets, very difficult to localize. You cannot point to it in the speeches; indeed, if you examine the two famous soliloquies you see the versification of Shakespeare, but a content which might be claimed by another, perhaps by the author of the *Revenge of Bussy d'Ambois,* Act V. sc. i. We find Shakespeare's *Hamlet* not in the action, not in any quotations that we might select, so much as in an unmistakable tone which is unmistakably not in the earlier play.

The only way of expressing emotion in the form of art is by finding an "objective correlative"; in other words, a set of objects, a situation, a chain of events which shall be the formula of that *particular* emotion; such that when the external facts, which must terminate in sensory experience, are given, the emotion is immediately evoked. If you examine any of Shakespeare's more successful tragedies, you will find this exact equivalence; you will find that the state of mind of Lady Macbeth walking in her sleep has been communicated to you by a skilful accumulation of imagined sensory impressions; the words of Macbeth on hearing of his wife's death strike us as if, given the sequence of events, these words were automatically released by the last event in the series. The artistic "inevitability" lies in this complete adequacy of the external to the emotion; and this is precisely what is deficient in *Hamlet.* Hamlet (the man) is dominated by an emotion which is inexpressible, because it is in *excess* of the facts as they appear. And the supposed identity of Hamlet with his author is genuine to this point: that Hamlet's bafflement at the absence of objective equivalent to his feelings is a prolongation of the bafflement of his creator in the face of his artistic problem. Hamlet is up against the difficulty that his disgust is occasioned by his mother, but that his mother is not an adequate equivalent for it; his disgust envelops and exceeds her. It is thus a feeling which he cannot understand; he cannot objectify it, and it therefore remains to poison life and obstruct action. None of the possible actions can satisfy it; and nothing that Shakespeare can do with the plot can express Hamlet for him. And it must be noticed that the very nature of the *donées* of the problem precludes objective equivalence. To have heightened the criminality of Gertrude would have been to provide the formula for a totally different emotion in Hamlet; it is just *because* her character is so negative and insignificant that she arouses in Hamlet the feeling which she is incapable of representing.

The "madness" of Hamlet lay to Shakespeare's hand; in the earlier play a simple ruse, and to the end, we may presume, understood as a ruse by the audience. For Shakespeare it is less than madness and more than feigned. The levity of Hamlet, his repetition of phrase, his puns, are not part of a deliberate plan of dissimulation, but a form of emotional relief. In the character Hamlet it is the buffoonery of an emotion which can find no outlet in action; in the dramatist it is the buffoonery of an emotion which he cannot express in art. The intense feeling, ecstatic or terrible, without an object or exceeding its object, is something which every person of sensibility has known; it is doubtless a study to pathologists. It often occurs in adolescence: the ordinary person puts these feelings to sleep, or trims down his feeling to fit the business world; the artist keeps it alive by his ability to intensify the world to his emotions. The Hamlet of Laforgue is an adolescent; the Hamlet of Shakespeare is not, he has not that explanation and excuse. We must simply admit that here Shakespeare tackled a problem which proved too much for him. Why he attempted it at all is an insoluble puzzle; under compulsion of what experience he attempted to express the inexpressibly horrible, we cannot ever know. We need a great many facts in his biography; and we should like to know whether, and when, and after or at the same time as what personal experience, he read Montaigne, II. xii., *Apologie de Raimond Sebond*. We should have, finally, to know something which is by hypothesis unknowable, for we assume it to be an experience which, in the manner indicated, exceeded the facts. We should have to understand things which Shakespeare did not understand himself.

# BEN JONSON

THE reputation of Jonson has been of the most deadly kind that can be compelled upon the memory of a great poet. To be universally accepted; to be damned by the praise that quenches all desire to read the book; to be afflicted by the imputation of the virtues which excite the least pleasure; and to be read only by historians and antiquaries—this is the most perfect conspiracy of approval. For some generations the reputation of Jonson has been carried rather as a liability than as an asset in the balance-sheet of English literature. No critic has succeeded in making him appear pleasurable or even interesting. Swinburne's book on Jonson satisfies no curiosity and stimulates no thought. For the critical study in the "Men of Letters Series" by Mr. Gregory Smith there is a place; it satisfies curiosity, it supplies many just observations, it provides valuable matter on the neglected masques; it only fails to remodel the image of Jonson which is settled in our minds. Probably the fault lies with several generations of our poets. It is not that the value of poetry is only its value to living poets for their own work; but appreciation is akin to creation, and true enjoyment of poetry is related to the stirring of suggestion, the stimulus that a poet feels in his enjoyment of other poetry. Jonson has provided no creative stimulus for a very long time; consequently we must look back as far as Dryden—precisely, a poetic practitioner who learned from Jonson—before we find a living criticism of Jonson's work.

Yet there are possibilities for Jonson even now. We have no difficulty in seeing what brought him to this pass; how, in contrast, not with Shakespeare, but with Marlowe, Webster, Donne, Beaumont, and Fletcher, he has been paid out with reputation instead of enjoyment. He is no less a poet than these men, but his poetry is of the surface. Poetry of the surface cannot be understood without study; for to deal with the surface of life, as Jonson dealt with it, is to deal so deliberately that we too must be deliberate, in order to understand. Shakespeare, and smaller men also, are in the end more difficult, but they offer something at the start to encourage the student or to satisfy those who want nothing more; they are suggestive, evocative, a phrase, a voice; they offer poetry in detail as well as in design. So does Dante offer something, a phrase everywhere *(tu se' ombra ed ombra vedi)* even to readers who have no Italian; and Dante and Shakespeare have poetry of design as well as of detail. But the polished veneer of Jonson reflects only the lazy reader's fatuity; unconscious does not respond to unconscious; no swarms of inarticulate feelings are aroused. The immediate appeal of Jonson is to the mind; his emotional tone is not in the single verse, but in the design of the whole. But not many people are capable of discovering for themselves the beauty which is only found after labour; and Jonson's industrious readers have been those whose interest was historical and curious, and those who have thought that in discovering the historical and curious interest they had discovered the artistic value as well. When we say that Jonson requires study, we do not mean study of his classical scholarship or of seventeenth-century manners. We mean intelligent saturation in his work as a whole; we mean that in order to enjoy him at all, we must get to the centre of his work and his temperament, and that we must see him unbiased by time, as a contemporary. And to see him as a contemporary does not so much require the power of putting ourselves into seventeenth-century London as it requires the power of setting Jonson in our London: a more difficult triumph of divination.

It is generally conceded that Jonson failed as a tragic dramatist; and it is usually agreed that he failed because his genius was for satiric comedy and because of the weight of pedantic learning with which he burdened his two tragic failures. The second point marks an obvious error of detail; the first is too crude a statement to be accepted; to say that he failed because his genius was unsuited to tragedy is to tell us nothing at all. Jonson did not write a good tragedy, but we can see no reason why he should not have written one. If two plays so different as *The Tempest* and *The Silent Woman* are both comedies, surely the category of tragedy could be made wide enough to include something possible for Jonson to have done. But the classification of tragedy and comedy, while it may be sufficient to mark the distinction in a dramatic literature of more rigid form and treatment—it may distinguish Aristophanes from Euripides—is not adequate to a drama of such variations as the Elizabethans. Tragedy is a crude classification for plays so different in their tone as *Macbeth, The Jew of Malta,* and *The Witch of Edmonton;* and it does not help us much to say that *The Merchant of Venice* and *The Alchemist* are comedies. Jonson had his own scale, his own instrument. The merit which *Catiline* possesses is the same merit that is exhibited more triumphantly in *Volpone; Catiline* fails,

not because it is too laboured and conscious, but because it is not conscious enough; because Jonson in this play was not alert to his own idiom,
not clear in his mind as to what his temperament wanted him to do. In
*Catiline* Jonson conforms, or attempts to conform, to conventions; not to
the conventions of antiquity, which he had exquisitely under control, but
to the conventions of tragico-historical drama of his time. It is not the
Latin erudition that sinks *Catiline,* but the application of that erudition to
a form which was not the proper vehicle for the mind which had amassed
the erudition.

If you look at *Catiline*—that dreary Pyrrhic victory of tragedy—you
find two passages to be successful: Act ii. scene I, the dialogue of the political ladies, and the Prologue of Sylla's ghost. These two passages are
genial. The soliloquy of the ghost is a characteristic Jonson success in
content and in versification—

> Dost thou not feel me, Rome? not yet! is night
> So heavy on thee, and my weight so light?
> Can Sylla's ghost arise within thy walls,
> Less threatening than an earthquake, the quick falls
> Of thee and thine? Shake not the frighted heads
> Of thy steep towers, or shrink to their first beds?
> Or as their ruin the large Tyber fills,
> Make that swell up, and drown thy seven proud hills? . . .

This is the learned, but also the creative, Jonson. Without concerning
himself with the character of Sulla, and in lines of invective, Jonson
makes Sylla's ghost, while the words are spoken, a living and terrible
force. The words fall with as determined beat as if they were the will of
the morose Dictator himself. You may say: merely invective; but mere
invective, even if as superior to the clumsy fisticuffs of Marston and Hall
as Jonson's verse is superior to theirs, would not create a living figure as
Jonson has done in this long tirade. And you may say: rhetoric; but if we
are to call it "rhetoric" we must subject that term to a closer dissection
than any to which it is accustomed. What Jonson has done here is not
merely a fine speech. It is the careful, precise filling in of a strong and
simple outline, and at no point does it overflow the outline; it is far more
careful and precise in its obedience to this outline than are many of the
speeches in *Tamburlaine.* The outline is not Sulla, for Sulla has nothing to
do with it, but "Sylla's ghost." The words may not be suitable to an historical Sulla, or to anybody in history, but they are a perfect expression
for "Sylla's ghost." You cannot say they are rhetorical "because people do
not talk like that," you cannot call them "verbiage"; they do not exhibit

prolixity or redundancy or the other vices in the rhetoric books; there is
a definite artistic emotion which demands expression at that length. The
words themselves are mostly simple words, the syntax is natural, the language austere rather than adorned. Turning then to the induction of *The
Poetaster*, we find another success of the same kind—

> Light, I salute thee, but with wounded nerves . . .

Men may not talk in that way, but the spirit of envy does, and in the
words of Jonson envy is a real and living person. It is not human life that
informs envy and Sylla's ghost, but it is energy of which human life is
only another variety.

Returning to *Catiline*, we find that the best scene in the body of the play
is one which cannot be squeezed into a tragic frame, and which appears
to belong to satiric comedy. The scene between Fulvia and Galla and
Sempronia is a living scene in a wilderness of oratory. And as it recalls
other scenes—there is a suggestion of the college of ladies in *The Silent
Woman*—it looks like a comedy scene. And it appears to be satire.

> They shall all give and pay well, that come here,
> If they will have it; and that, jewels, pearl,
> Plate, or round sums to buy these. I'm not taken
> With a cob-swan or a high-mounting bull,
> As foolish Leda and Europa were;
> But the bright gold, with Danaë. For such price
> I would endure a rough, harsh Jupiter,
> Or ten such thundering gamesters, and refrain
> To laugh at 'em, till they are gone, with my much suffering.

This scene is no more comedy than it is tragedy, and the "satire" is merely
a medium for the essential emotion. Jonson's drama is only incidentally
satire, because it is only incidentally a criticism upon the actual world. It
is not satire in the way in which the work of Swift or the work of Molière
may be called satire: that is, it does not find its source in any precise emotional attitude or precise intellectual criticism of the actual world. It is
satire perhaps as the work of Rabelais is satire; certainly not more so. The
important thing is that if fiction can be divided into creative fiction and
critical fiction, Jonson's is creative. That he was a great critic, our first
great critic, does not affect this assertion. Every creator is also a critic;
Jonson was a conscious critic, but he was also conscious in his creations.
Certainly, one sense in which the term "critical" may be applied to fiction
is a sense in which the term might be used of a method antithetical to

Jonson's. It is the method of *Education Sentimentale*. The characters of
Jonson, of Shakespeare, perhaps of all the greatest drama, are drawn in
positive and simple outlines. They may be filled in, and by Shakespeare
they are filled in, by much detail or many shifting aspects; but a clear and
sharp and simple form remains through these—though it would be hard
to say in what the clarity and sharpness and simplicity of Hamlet consists.
But Frédéric Moreau is not made in that way. He is constructed partly by
negative definition, built up by a great number of observations. We cannot isolate him from the environment in which we find him; it may be an
environment which is or can be much universalized; nevertheless it, and
the figure in it, consist of very many observed particular facts, the actual
world. Without this world the figure dissolves. The ruling faculty is a
critical perception, a commentary upon experienced feeling and sensation. If this is true of Flaubert, it is true in a higher degree of Molière
than of Jonson. The broad farcical lines of Molière may seem to be the
same drawing as Jonson's. But Molière—say in Alceste or Monsieur
Jourdain—is criticizing the actual; the reference to the actual world is
more direct. And having a more tenuous reference, the work of Jonson is
much less directly satirical.

This leads us to the question of Humours. Largely on the evidence of
the two Humour plays, it is sometimes assumed that Jonson is occupied
with types; typical exaggerations, or exaggerations of type. The Humour
definition, the expressed intention of Jonson, may be satisfactory for these
two plays. *Every Man in his Humour* is the first mature work of Jonson, and
the student of Jonson must study it; but it is not the play in which Jonson
found his genius: it is the last of his plays to read first. If one reads *Volpone*,
and after that re-reads the *Jew of Malta*; then returns to Jonson and reads
*Bartholomew Fair, The Alchemist, Epicœne* and *The Devil is an Ass*, and finally
*Catiline*, it is possible to arrive at a fair opinion of the poet and the dramatist.

The Humour, even at the beginning, is not a type, as in Marston's
satire, but a simplified and somewhat distorted individual with a typical
mania. In the later work, the Humour definition quite fails to account for
the total effect produced. The characters of Shakespeare are such as
might exist in different circumstances than those in which Shakespeare
sets them. The latter appear to be those which extract from the characters the most intense and interesting realization; but that realization has
not exhausted their possibilities. Volpone's life, on the other hand, is
bounded by the scene in which it is played; in fact, the life is the life of
the scene and is derivatively the life of Volpone; the life of the character

is inseparable from the life of the drama. This is not dependence upon a background, or upon a substratum of fact. The emotional effect is single and simple. Whereas in Shakespeare the effect is due to the way in which the characters *act upon* one another, in Jonson it is given by the way in which the characters *fit in* with each other. The artistic result of *Volpone* is not due to any effect that Volpone, Mosca, Corvino, Corbaccio, Voltore have upon each other, but simply to their combination into a whole. And these figures are not personifications of passions; separately, they have not even that reality, they are constituents. It is a similar indication of Jonson's method that you can hardly pick out a line of Jonson's and say confidently that it is great poetry; but there are many extended passages to which you cannot deny that honour.

> I will have all my beds blown up, not stuft;
> Down is too hard; and then, mine oval room
> Fill'd with such pictures as Tiberius took
> From Elephantis, and dull Aretine
> But coldly imitated. Then, my glasses
> Cut in more subtle angles, to disperse
> And multiply the figures, as I walk. . . .

Jonson is the legitimate heir of Marlowe. The man who wrote, in *Volpone:*

> for thy love,
> In varying figures, I would have contended
> With the blue Proteus, or the hornèd flood. . . .

and

> See, a carbuncle
> May put out both the eyes of our Saint Mark;
> A diamond would have bought Lollia Paulina,
> When she came in like star-light, hid with jewels. . . .

is related to Marlowe as a poet; and if Marlowe is a poet, Jonson is also. And, if Jonson's comedy is a comedy of humours, then Marlowe's tragedy, a large part of it, is a tragedy of humours. But Jonson has too exclusively been considered as the typical representative of a point of view toward comedy. He has suffered from his great reputation as a critic and theorist, from the effects of his intelligence. We have been taught to think of him as the man, the dictator (confusedly in our minds with his later name-sake), as the literary politician impressing his views upon a generation; we are offended by the constant reminder of his scholarship. We forget the comedy in the humours, and the serious artist in the scholar. Jonson has suffered in public opinion, as anyone must suffer who is forced to talk about his art.

If you examine the first hundred lines or more of *Volpone* the verse appears to be in the manner of Marlowe, more deliberate, more mature, but without Marlowe's inspiration. It looks like mere "rhetoric," certainly not "deeds and language such as men do use"! It appears to us, in fact, forced and flagitious bombast. That it is not "rhetoric," or at least not vicious rhetoric, we do not know until we are able to review the whole play. For the consistent maintenance of this manner conveys in the end an effect not of verbosity, but of bold, even shocking and terrifying directness. We have difficulty in saying exactly what produces this simple and single effect. It is not in any ordinary way due to management of intrigue. Jonson employs immense dramatic constructive skill: it is not so much skill in plot as skill in doing without a plot. He never manipulates as complicated a plot as that of *The Merchant of Venice*; he has in his best plays nothing like the intrigue of Restoration comedy. In *Bartholomew Fair* it is hardly a plot at all; the marvel of the play is the bewildering rapid chaotic action of the fair; it is the fair itself, not anything that happens to take place in the fair. In *Volpone*, or *The Alchemist*, or *The Silent Woman*, the plot is enough to keep the players in motion; it is rather an "action" than a plot. The plot does not hold the play together; what holds the play together is a unity of inspiration that radiates into plot and personages alike.

We have attempted to make more precise the sense in which it was said that Jonson's work is "of the surface"; carefully avoiding the word "superficial." For there is work contemporary with Jonson's which is superficial in a pejorative sense in which the word cannot be applied to Jonson—the work of Beaumont and Fletcher. If we look at the work of Jonson's great contemporaries, Shakespeare, and also Donne and Webster and Tourneur (and sometimes Middleton), have a depth, a third dimension, as Mr. Gregory Smith rightly calls it, which Jonson's work has not. Their words have often a network of tentacular roots reaching down to the deepest terrors and desires. Jonson's most certainly have not; but in Beaumont and Fletcher we may think that at times we find it. Looking closer, we discover that the blossoms of Beaumont and Fletcher's imagination draw no sustenance from the soil, but are cut and slightly withered flowers stuck into sand.

Wilt thou, hereafter, when they talk of me,
As thou shalt hear nothing but infamy,
Remember some of these things? . . .
I pray thee, do; for thou shalt never see me so again.

Hair woven in many a curious warp,
Able in endless error to enfold
The wandering soul; . . .

Detached from its context, this looks like the verse of the greater poets;
just as lines of Jonson, detached from their context, look like inflated or
empty fustian. But the evocative quality of the verse of Beaumont and
Fletcher depends upon a clever appeal to emotions and associations
which they have not themselves grasped; it is hollow. It is superficial with
a vacuum behind it; the superficies of Jonson is solid. It is what it is; it
does not pretend to be another thing. But it is so very conscious and
deliberate that we must look with eyes alert to the whole before we
apprehend the significance of any part. We cannot call a man's work
superficial when it is the creation of a world; a man cannot be accused of
dealing superficially with the world which he himself has created; the
superficies *is* the world. Jonson's characters conform to the logic of the
emotions of their world. It is a world like Lobatchevsky's; the worlds created by artists like Jonson are like systems of non-Euclidean geometry.
They are not fancy, because they have a logic of their own; and this logic
illuminates the actual world, because it gives us a new point of view from
which to inspect it.

A writer of power and intelligence, Jonson endeavoured to promulgate,
as a formula and programme of reform, what he chose to do himself; and
he not unnaturally laid down in abstract theory what is in reality a personal point of view. And it is in the end of no value to discuss Jonson's
theory and practice unless we recognize and seize this point of view,
which escapes the formulæ, and which is what makes his plays worth
reading. Jonson behaved as the great creative mind that he was: he created his own world, a world from which his followers, as well as the dramatists who were trying to do something wholly different, are excluded.
Remembering this, we turn to Mr. Gregory Smith's objection—that
Jonson's characters lack the third dimension, have no life out of the theatrical existence in which they appear—and demand an inquest. The
objection implies that the characters are purely the work of intellect,
or the result of superficial observation of a world which is faded or
mildewed. It implies that the characters are lifeless. But if we dig beneath
the theory, beneath the observation, beneath the deliberate drawing and

the theatrical and dramatic elaboration, there is discovered a kind of power, animating Volpone, Busy, Fitzdottrel, the literary ladies of *Epicœne*, even Bobadil, which comes from below the intellect, and for which no theory of humours will account. And it is the same kind of power which vivifies Trimalchio, and Panurge, and some but not all of the "comic" characters of Dickens. The fictive life of this kind is not to be circumscribed by a reference to "comedy" or to "farce"; it is not exactly the kind of life which informs the characters of Molière or that which informs those of Marivaux—two writers who were, besides, doing something quite different the one from the other. But it is something which distinguishes Barabas from Shylock, Epicure Mammon from Falstaff, Faustus from—if you will—Macbeth; Marlowe and Jonson from Shakespeare and the Shakespearians, Webster, and Tourneur. It is not merely Humours: for neither Volpone nor Mosca is a humour. No theory of humours could account for Jonson's best plays or the best characters in them. We want to know at what point the comedy of humours passes into a work of art, and why Jonson is not Brome.

The creation of a work of art, we will say the creation of a character in a drama, consists in the process of transfusion of the personality, or, in a deeper sense, the life, of the author into the character. This is a very different matter from the orthodox creation in one's own image. The ways in which the passions and desires of the creator may be satisfied in the work of art are complex and devious. In a painter they may take the form of a predilection for certain colours, tones, or lightings; in a writer the original impulse may be even more strangely transmuted. Now, we may say with Mr. Gregory Smith that Falstaff or a score of Shakespeare's characters have a "third dimension" that Jonson's have not. This will mean, not that Shakespeare's spring from the feelings or imagination and Jonson's from the intellect or invention; they have equally an emotional source; but that Shakespeare's represent a more complex tissue of feelings and desires, as well as a more supple, a more susceptible temperament. Falstaff is not only the roast Malmesbury ox with the pudding in his belly; he also "grows old," and, finally, his nose is as sharp as a pen. He was perhaps the *satisfaction* of more, and of more complicated feelings; and perhaps he was, as the great tragic characters must have been, the offspring of deeper, less apprehensible feelings: deeper, but not necessarily stronger or more intense, than those of Jonson. It is obvious that the spring of the difference is not the difference between feeling and thought, or superior insight, superior perception, on the part of Shakespeare, but his susceptibility to a greater range of emotion, and emotion deeper and more obscure. But his characters are no more "alive" than are the characters of Jonson.

The world they live in is a larger one. But small worlds—the worlds which artists create—do not differ only in magnitude; if they are complete worlds, drawn to scale in every part, they differ in kind also. And Jonson's world has this scale. His type of personality found its relief in something falling under the category of burlesque or farce—though when you are dealing with a *unique* world, like his, these terms fail to appease the desire for definition. It is not, at all events, the farce of Molière: the latter is more analytic, more an intellectual redistribution. It is not defined by the word "satire." Jonson poses as a satirist. But satire like Jonson's is great in the end not by hitting off its object, but by creating it; the satire is merely the means which leads to the æsthetic result, the impulse which projects a new world into a new orbit. In *Every Man in his Humour* there is a neat, a very neat, comedy of humours. In discovering and proclaiming in this play the new genre Jonson was simply recognizing, unconsciously, the route which opened out in the proper direction for his instincts. His characters are and remain, like Marlowe's, simplified characters; but the simplification does not consist in the dominance of a particular humour or monomania. That is a very superficial account of it. The simplification consists largely in reduction of detail, in the seizing of aspects relevant to the relief of an emotional impulse which remains the same for that character, in making the character conform to a particular setting. This stripping is essential to the art, to which is also essential a flat distortion in the drawing; it is an art of caricature, of great caricature, like Marlowe's. It is a great caricature, which is beautiful; and a great humour, which is serious. The "world" of Jonson is sufficiently large; it is a world of poetic imagination; it is sombre. He did not get the third dimension, but he was not trying to get it.

If we approach Jonson with less frozen awe of his learning, with a clearer understanding of his "rhetoric" and its applications, if we grasp the fact that the knowledge required of the reader is not archæology but knowledge of Jonson, we can derive not only instruction in non-Euclidean humanity—but enjoyment. We can even apply him, be aware of him as a part of our literary inheritance craving further expression. Of all the dramatists of his time, Jonson is probably the one whom the present age would find the most sympathetic, if it knew him. There is a brutality, a lack of sentiment, a polished surface, a handling of large bold designs in brilliant colours, which ought to attract about three thousand people in London and elsewhere. At least, if we had a contemporary Shakespeare and a contemporary Jonson, it would be the Jonson who would arouse the enthusiasm of the intelligentsia! Though he is saturated in literature, he never sacrifices the theatrical qualities—theatrical in the most favourable sense—to literature or to the study of character. His work is a titanic show. But Jonson's masques, an important part of his work, are neglected; our flaccid culture lets shows and literature fade, but prefers faded literature to faded shows. There are hundreds of people who have read *Comus* to ten who have read the *Masque of Blackness*. *Comus* contains fine poetry, and poetry exemplifying some merits to which Jonson's masque poetry cannot pretend. Nevertheless, *Comus* is the death of the masque; it is the transition of a form of art—even of a form which existed for but a short generation—into "literature," literature cast in a form which has lost its application. Even though *Comus* was a masque at Ludlow Castle, Jonson had, what Milton came perhaps too late to have, a sense for living art; his art was applied. The masques can still be read, and with pleasure, by anyone who will take the trouble—a trouble which in this part of Jonson is, indeed, a study of antiquities—to imagine them in action, displayed with the music, costume, dances, and the scenery of Inigo Jones. They are additional evidence that Jonson had a fine sense of form, of the purpose for which a particular form is intended; evidence that he was a literary artist even more than he was a man of letters.

# PHILIP MASSINGER

## I

MASSINGER has been more fortunately and more fairly judged than several of his greater contemporaries. Three critics have done their best by him: the notes of Coleridge exemplify Coleridge's fragmentary and fine perceptions; the essay of Leslie Stephen is a piece of formidable destructive analysis; and the essay of Swinburne is Swinburne's criticism at its best. None of these, probably, has put Massinger finally and irrefutably into a place.

English criticism is inclined to argue or persuade rather than to state; and, instead of forcing the subject to expose himself, these critics have left in their work an undissolved residuum of their own good taste, which, however impeccable, is something that requires our faith. The principles which animate this taste remain unexplained. Mr. Cruickshank's book is a work of scholarship; and the advantage of good scholarship is that it presents us with evidence which is an invitation to the critical faculty of the reader: it bestows a method, rather than a judgment.

It is difficult—it is perhaps the supreme difficulty of criticism—to make the facts generalize themselves; but Mr. Cruickshank at least presents us with facts which are capable of generalization. This is a service of value; and it is therefore wholly a compliment to the author to say that his appendices are as valuable as the essay itself.

The sort of labour to which Mr. Cruickshank has devoted himself is one that professed critics ought more willingly to undertake. It is an important part of criticism, more important than any mere expression of opinion. To understand Elizabethan drama it is necessary to study a dozen playwrights at once, to dissect with all care the complex growth, to ponder collaboration to the utmost line. Reading Shakespeare and several of his contemporaries is pleasure enough, perhaps all the pleasure possible, for most. But if we wish to consummate and refine this pleasure by understanding it, to distill the last drop of it, to press and press the essence of each author, to apply exact measurement to our own sensations, then we must compare; and we cannot compare without parcelling the threads of authorship and influence. We must employ Mr. Cruickshank's method to examine Mr. Cruickshank's judgments; and perhaps the most important judgment to which he has committed himself is this:—

> Massinger, in his grasp of stagecraft, his flexible metre, his desire in the sphere of ethics to exploit both vice and virtue, is typical of an age which had much culture, but which, without being exactly corrupt, lacked moral fibre.

Here, in fact, is our text: to elucidate this sentence would be to account for Massinger. We begin vaguely with good taste, by a recognition that Massinger is inferior: can we trace this inferiority, dissolve it, and have left any element of merit?

We turn first to the parallel quotations from Massinger and Shakespeare collocated by Mr. Cruickshank to make manifest Massinger's indebtedness. One of the surest of tests is the way in which a poet borrows. Immature poets imitate; mature poets steal; bad poets deface what they take, and good poets make it into something better, or at least something different. The good poet welds his theft into a whole of feeling which is unique, utterly different from that from which it was torn; the bad poet throws it into something which has no cohesion. A good poet will usually borrow from authors remote in time, or alien in language, or diverse in interest. Chapman borrowed from Seneca; Shakespeare and Webster from Montaigne. The two great followers of Shakespeare, Webster and Tourneur, in their mature work do not borrow from him; he is too close to them to be of use to them in this way. Massinger, as Mr. Cruickshank shows, borrows from Shakespeare a good deal. Let us profit by some of the quotations with which he has provided us—

> *Massinger:* Can I call back yesterday, with all their aids
> That bow unto my sceptre? or restore
> My mind to that tranquillity and peace
> It then enjoyed?

> *Shakespeare:* Not poppy, nor mandragora,
> Nor all the drowsy syrops of the world
> Shall ever medecine thee to that sweet sleep
> Which thou owedst yesterday.

Massinger's is a general rhetorical question, the language just and pure, but colourless. Shakespeare's has particular significance; and the adjective "drowsy" and the verb "medecine" infuse a precise vigour. This is, on Massinger's part, an echo rather than an imitation or a plagiarism—the basest, because least conscious form of borrowing. "Drowsy syrop" is a condensation of meaning frequent in Shakespeare, but rare in Massinger.

> *Massinger:* Thou didst not borrow of Vice her indirect,
>     Crooked, and abject means.

> *Shakespeare:* God knows, my son,
>     By what by-paths and indirect crook'd ways
>     I met this crown.

Here, again, Massinger gives the general forensic statement, Shakespeare the particular image. "Indirect crook'd" is forceful in Shakespeare; a mere pleonasm in Massinger. "Crook'd ways" is a metaphor; Massinger's phrase only the ghost of a metaphor.

> *Massinger:* And now, in the evening,
>     When thou shoud'st pass with honour to thy rest,
>     Wilt thou fall like a meteor?

> *Shakespeare:* I shall fall
>     Like a bright exhalation in the evening,
>     And no man see me more.

Here the lines of Massinger have their own beauty. Still, a "bright exhalation" appears to the eye and makes us catch our breath in the evening; "meteor" is a dim simile; the word is worn.

> *Massinger:* What you deliver to me shall be lock'd up
>     In a strong cabinet, of which you yourself
>     Shall keep the key.

> *Shakespeare:* 'Tis in my memory locked,
>     And you yourself shall keep the key of it.

In the preceding passage Massinger had squeezed his simile to death, here he drags it round the city at his heels; and how swift Shakespeare's figure is! We may add two more passages, not given by our commentator; here the model is Webster. They occur on the same page, an artless confession.

> Here he comes,
> His nose held up; he hath something in the wind,

is hardly comparable to "the Cardinal lifts up his nose like a foul porpoise before a storm," and when we come upon

> as tann'd galley-slaves
> Pay such as do redeem them from the oar

it is unnecessary to turn up the great lines in the *Duchess of Malfi*. Massinger fancied this galley-slave; for he comes with his oar again in the *Bondsman*—

> Never did galley-slave shake off his chains,
> Or looked on his redemption from the oar. . . .

Now these are mature plays; and the *Roman Actor* (from which we have drawn the two previous extracts) is said to have been the preferred play of its author.

We may conclude directly from these quotations that Massinger's feeling for language had outstripped his feeling for things; that his eye and his vocabulary were not in close co-operation. One of the greatest distinctions of several of his elder contemporaries—we name Middleton, Webster, Tourneur—is a gift for combining, for fusing into a single phrase, two or more diverse impressions.

> . . . . in her strong toil of grace

of Shakespeare is such a fusion; the metaphor identifies itself with what suggests it; the resultant is one and is unique—

> Does the silk worm *expend* her *yellow labours?* . . .
> Why does yon fellow *falsify highways*
> And lays his life between the judge's lips
> To *refine* such a one? keeps horse and men
> To *beat their valours* for her?
>
> Let the common sewer take it from distinction. . . .
> Lust and forgetfulness have been amongst us. . . .

These lines of Tourneur and of Middleton exhibit that perpetual slight alteration of language, words perpetually juxtaposed in new and sudden combinations, meanings perpetually *eingeschachtelt* into meanings, which evidences a very high development of the senses, a development of the English language which we have perhaps never equalled. And, indeed, with the end of Chapman, Middleton, Webster, Tourneur, Donne we end a period when the intellect was immediately at the tips of the senses. Sensation became word and the word was sensation. The next period is the period of Milton (though still with a Marvell in it); and this period is initiated by Massinger.

It is not that the word becomes less exact. Massinger is, in a wholly eulogistic sense, choice and correct. And the decay of the senses is not inconsistent with a greater sophistication of language. But every vital development in language is a development of feeling as well. The verse of Shakespeare and the major Shakespearian dramatists is an innovation of this kind, a true mutation of species. The verse practised by Massinger is a different verse from that of his predecessors; but it is not a development based on, or resulting from, a new way of feeling. On the contrary, it seems to lead us away from feeling altogether.

We mean that Massinger must be placed as much at the beginning of one period as at the end of another. A certain Boyle, quoted by Mr. Cruickshank, says that Milton's blank verse owes much to the study of Massinger's.

> In the indefinable touches which make up the music of a verse [says Boyle], in the artistic distribution of pauses, and in the unerring choice and grouping of just those words which strike the ear as the perfection of harmony, there are, if we leave Cyril Tourneur's *Atheist's Tragedy* out of the question, only two masters in the drama, Shakespeare in his latest period and Massinger.

This Boyle must have had a singular ear to have preferred Tourneur's apprentice work to his *Revenger's Tragedy,* and one must think that he had never glanced at Ford. But though the appraisal be ludicrous, the praise is not undeserved. Mr. Cruickshank has given us an excellent example of Massinger's syntax—

> What though my father
> Writ man before he was so, and confirm'd it,
> By numbering that day no part of his life
> In which he did not service to his country;

> Was he to be free therefore from the laws
> And ceremonious form in your decrees?
> Or else because he did as much as man
> In those three memorable overthrows,
> At Granson, Morat, Nancy, where his master,
> The warlike Charalois, with whose misfortunes
> I bear his name, lost treasure, men, and life,
> To be excused from payment of those sums
> Which (his own patrimony spent) his zeal
> To serve his country forced him to take up!

It is impossible to deny the masterly construction of this passage; perhaps there is not one living poet who could do the like. It is impossible to deny the originality. The language is pure and correct, free from muddiness or turbidity. Massinger does not confuse metaphors, or heap them one upon another. He is lucid, though not easy. But if Massinger's age, "without being exactly corrupt, lacks moral fibre," Massinger's verse, without being exactly corrupt, suffers from cerebral anæmia. To say that an involved style is necessarily a bad style would be preposterous. But such a style should follow the involutions of a mode of perceiving, registering, and digesting impressions which is also involved. It is to be feared that the feeling of Massinger is simple and overlaid with received ideas. Had Massinger had a nervous system as refined as that of Middleton, Tourneur, Webster, or Ford, his style would be a triumph. But such a nature was not at hand, and Massinger precedes, not another Shakespeare, but Milton.

Massinger is, in fact, at a further remove from Shakespeare than that other precursor of Milton—John Fletcher. Fletcher was above all an opportunist, in his verse, in his momentary effects, never quite a pastiche; in his structure ready to sacrifice everything to the single scene. To Fletcher, because he was more intelligent, less will be forgiven. Fletcher had a cunning guess at feelings, and betrayed them; Massinger was unconscious and innocent. As an artisan of the theatre he is not inferior to Fletcher, and his best tragedies have an honester unity than *Bonduca*. But the unity is superficial. In the *Roman Actor* the development of parts is out of all proportion to the central theme; in the *Unnatural Combat*, in spite of the deft handling of suspense and the quick shift from climax to a new suspense, the first part of the play is the hatred of Malefort for his son and the second part is his passion for his daughter. It is theatrical skill, not an artistic conscience arranging emotions, that holds the two parts together. In the *Duke of Milan* the appearance of Sforza at the Court of his conqueror only delays the action, or rather breaks the emotional rhythm. And we have named three of Massinger's best.

A dramatist who so skilfully welds together parts which have no reason for being together, who fabricates plays so well knit and so remote from unity, we should expect to exhibit the same synthetic cunning in character. Mr. Cruickshank, Coleridge, and Leslie Stephen are pretty well agreed that Massinger is no master of characterization. You can, in fact, put together heterogeneous parts to form a lively play; but a character, to be living, must be conceived from some emotional unity. A character is not to be composed of scattered observations of human nature, but of parts which are felt together. Hence it is that although Massinger's failure to draw a moving character is no greater than his failure to make a whole play, and probably springs from the same defective sensitiveness, yet the failure in character is more conspicuous and more disastrous. A "living" character is not necessarily "true to life." It is a person whom we can see and hear, whether he be true or false to human nature as we know it. What the creator of character needs is not so much knowledge of motives as keen sensibility; the dramatist need not understand people; but he must be exceptionally aware of them. This awareness was not given to Massinger. He inherits the traditions of conduct, female chastity, hymeneal sanctity, the fashion of honour, without either criticizing or informing them from his own experience. In the earlier drama these conventions are merely a framework, or an alloy necessary for working the metal; the metal itself consisted of unique emotions resulting inevitably from the circumstances, resulting or inhering as inevitably as the properties of a chemical compound. Middleton's heroine, for instance, in the *Changeling*, exclaims in the well-known words—

> Why, 'tis impossible thou canst be so wicked,
> To shelter such a cunning cruelty
> To make his death the murderer of my honour!

The word "honour" in such a situation is out of date, but the emotion of Beatrice at that moment, given the conditions, is as permanent and substantial as anything in human nature. The emotion of Othello in Act v. is the emotion of a man who discovers that the worst part of his own soul has been exploited by some one more clever than he; it is this emotion carried by the writer to a very high degree of intensity. Even in so late and so decayed a drama as that of Ford, the framework of emotions and morals of the time is only the vehicle for statements of feeling which are unique and imperishable: Ford's and Ford's only.

What may be considered corrupt or decadent in the morals of Massinger is not an alteration or diminution in morals; it is simply the disappearance of all the personal and real emotions which this morality supported and into which it introduced a kind of order. As soon as the emotions disappear the morality which ordered it appears hideous. Puritanism itself became repulsive only when it appeared as the survival of a restraint after the feelings which it restrained had gone. When Massinger's ladies resist temptation they do not appear to undergo any important emotion; they merely know what is expected of them; they manifest themselves to us as lubricious prudes. Any age has its conventions; and any age might appear absurd when its conventions get into the hands of a man like Massinger—a man, we mean, of so exceptionally superior a literary talent as Massinger's, and so paltry an imagination. The Elizabethan morality was an important convention; important because it was not consciously of one social class alone, because it provided a framework for emotions to which all classes could respond, and it hindered no feeling. It was not hypocritical, and it did not suppress; its dark corners are haunted by the ghosts of Mary Fitton and perhaps greater. It is a subject which has not been sufficiently investigated. Fletcher and Massinger rendered it ridiculous; not by not believing in it, but because they were men of great talents who could not vivify it; because they could not fit into it passionate, complete human characters.

The tragedy of Massinger is interesting chiefly according to the definition given before; the highest degree of verbal excellence compatible with the most rudimentary development of the senses. Massinger succeeds better in something which is not tragedy; in the romantic comedy. *A Very Woman* deserves all the praise that Swinburne, with his almost unerring gift for selection, has bestowed upon it. The probable collaboration of Fletcher had the happiest result; for certainly that admirable comic personage, the tipsy Borachia, is handled with more humour than we expect of Massinger. It is a play which would be enjoyable on the stage. The form, however, of romantic comedy is itself inferior and decadent. There is an inflexibility about the poetic drama which is by no means a matter of classical, or neoclassical, or pseudo-classical law. The poetic drama might develop forms highly different from those of Greece or England, India or Japan. Conceded the utmost freedom, the romantic drama would yet remain inferior. The poetic drama must have an emotional unity, let the emotion be whatever you like. It must have a dominant tone; and if this be strong enough, the most heterogeneous emotions may be made to reinforce it. The romantic comedy is a skilful concoction of inconsistent emotion, a *revue* of emotion. *A Very Woman* is surpassingly well plotted. The debility of romantic drama does not depend upon extravagant setting, or preposterous events, or inconceivable coincidences;

all these might be found in a serious tragedy or comedy. It consists in an internal incoherence of feelings, a concatenation of emotions which signifies nothing.

From this type of play, so eloquent of emotional disorder, there was no swing back of the pendulum. Changes never come by a simple reinfusion into the form which the life has just left. The romantic drama was not a new form. Massinger dealt not with emotions so much as with the social abstractions of emotions, more generalized and therefore more quickly and easily interchangeable within the confines of a single action. He was not guided by direct communications through the nerves. Romantic drama tended, accordingly, toward what is sometimes called the "typical," but which is not the truly typical; for the *typical* figure in a drama is always particularized—an individual. The tendency of the romantic drama was toward a form which continued it in removing its more conspicuous vices, was toward a more severe external order. This form was the Heroic Drama. We look into Dryden's "Essay on Heroic Plays," and we find that "love and valour ought to be the subject of an heroic poem." Massinger, in his destruction of the old drama, had prepared the way for Dryden. The intellect had perhaps exhausted the old conventions. It was not able to supply the impoverishment of feeling.

Such are the reflections aroused by an examination of some of Massinger's plays in the light of Mr. Cruickshank's statement that Massinger's age "had much culture, but, without being exactly corrupt, lacked moral fibre." The statement may be supported. In order to fit into our estimate of Massinger the two admirable comedies—*A New Way to Pay Old Debts* and *The City Madam*—a more extensive research would be required than is possible within our limits.

## II

Massinger's tragedy may be summarized for the unprepared reader as being very dreary. It is dreary, unless one is prepared by a somewhat extensive knowledge of his livelier contemporaries to grasp without fatigue precisely the elements in it which are capable of giving pleasure; or unless one is incited by a curious interest in versification. In comedy, however, Massinger was one of the few masters in the language. He was a master in a comedy which is serious, even sombre; and in one aspect of it there are only two names to mention with his: those of Marlowe and Jonson. In comedy, as a matter of fact, a greater variety of methods were discovered and employed than in tragedy. The method of Kyd, as developed by Shakespeare, was the standard for English tragedy down to

Otway and to Shelley. But both individual temperament, and varying epochs, made more play with comedy. The comedy of Lyly is one thing; that of Shakespeare, followed by Beaumont and Fletcher, is another; and that of Middleton is a third. And Massinger, while he has his own comedy, is nearer to Marlowe and Jonson than to any of these.

Massinger was, in fact, as a comic writer, fortunate in the moment at which he wrote. His comedy is transitional; but it happens to be one of those transitions which contain some merit not anticipated by predecessors or refined upon by later writers. The comedy of Jonson is nearer to caricature; that of Middleton a more photographic delineation of low life. Massinger is nearer to Restoration comedy, and more like his contemporary, Shirley, in assuming a certain social level, certain distinctions of class, as a postulate of his comedy. This resemblance to later comedy is also the important point of difference between Massinger and earlier comedy. But Massinger's comedy differs just as widely from the comedy of manners proper; he is closer to that in his romantic drama—in *A Very Woman*—than in *A New Way to Pay Old Debts;* in his comedy his interest is not in the follies of love-making or the absurdities of social pretence, but in the unmasking of villainy. Just as the Old Comedy of Molière differs in principle from the New Comedy of Marivaux, so the Old Comedy of Massinger differs from the New Comedy of his contemporary Shirley. And as in France, so in England, the more farcical comedy was the more serious. Massinger's great comic rogues, Sir Giles Overreach and Luke Frugal, are members of the large English family which includes Barabas and Sir Epicure Mammon, and from which Sir Tunbelly Clumsy claims descent.

What distinguishes Massinger from Marlowe and Jonson is in the main an inferiority. The greatest comic characters of these two dramatists are slight work in comparison with Shakespeare's best—Falstaff has a third dimension and Epicure Mammon has only two. But this slightness is part of the nature of the art which Jonson practised, a smaller art than Shakespeare's. The inferiority of Massinger to Jonson is an inferiority, not of one type of art to another, but within Jonson's type. It is a simple deficiency. Marlowe's and Jonson's comedies were a view of life; they were, as great literature is, the transformation of a personality into a personal work of art, their lifetime's work, long or short. Massinger is not simply a smaller personality: his personality hardly exists. He did not, out of his own personality, build a world of art, as Shakespeare and Marlowe and Jonson built.

In the fine pages which Remy de Gourmont devotes to Flaubert in his *Problème du Style,* the great critic declares:

La vie est un dépouillement. Le but de l'activité propre de
l'homme est de nettoyer sa personnalité, de la laver de toutes les
souillures qu'y déposa l'éducation, de la dégager de toutes les
empreintes qu'y laissèrent nos admirations adolescentes;

and again:

Flaubert incorporait toute sa sensibilité à ses œuvres. . . . Hors de
ses livres, où il se transvasait goutte à goutte, jusqu'à la lie, Flaubert
est fort peu intéressant. . . .

Of Shakespeare notably, of Jonson less, of Marlowe (and of Keats to the
term of life allowed him), one can say that they *se transvasaient goutte à
goutte;* and in England, which has produced a prodigious number of men
of genius and comparatively few works of art, there are not many writers
of whom one can say it. Certainly not of Massinger. A brilliant master of
technique, he was not, in this profound sense, an artist. And so we come
to inquire how, if this is so, he could have written two great comedies. We
shall probably be obliged to conclude that a large part of their excellence
is, in some way which should be defined, fortuitous; and that therefore
they are, however remarkable, not works of perfect art.

This objection raised by Leslie Stephen to Massinger's method of
revealing a villain has great cogency; but I am inclined to believe that the
cogency is due to a somewhat different reason from that which Leslie
Stephen assigns. His statement if too *apriorist* to be quite trustworthy.
There is no reason why a comedy or tragedy villain should not declare
himself, and in as long a period as the author likes; but the sort of villain
who may run on in this way is a simple villain (simple not *simpliste*).
Barabas and Volpone can declare their character, because they have no
inside; appearance and reality are coincident; they are forces in particular directions. Massinger's two villains are not simple. Giles Overreach is
essentially a great force directed upon small objects; a great force, a small
mind; the terror of a dozen parishes instead of the conqueror of a world.
The force is misapplied, attenuated, thwarted, by the man's vulgarity: he
is a great man of the City, without fear, but with the most abject awe of
the aristocracy. He is accordingly not simple, but a product of a certain
civilization, and he is not wholly conscious His monologues are meant to
be, not what he thinks he is, but what he really is: and yet they are not the
truth about him, and he himself certainly does not know the truth. To
declare himself, therefore, is impossible.

Nay, when my ears are pierced with widows' cries,
And undone orphans wash with tears my threshold,
I only think what 'tis to have my daughter
Right honourable; and 'tis a powerful charm
Makes me insensible of remorse, or pity,
Or the least sting of conscience.

This is the wrong note. Elsewhere we have the right:

Thou art a fool;
In being out of office, I am out of danger;
Where, if I were a justice, besides the trouble,
I might or out of wilfulness, or error,
Run myself finely into a praemunire,
And so become a prey to the informer,
No, I'll have none of't; 'tis enough I keep
Greedy at my devotion: so he serve
My purposes, let him hang, or damn, I care not . . .

And how well tuned, well modulated, here, the diction! The man is audible and visible. But from passages like the first we may be permitted to infer that Massinger was unconscious of trying to develop a different kind of character from any that Marlowe or Jonson had invented.

Luke Frugal, in *The City Madam,* is not so great a character as Sir Giles Overreach. But Luke Frugal just misses being almost the greatest of all hypocrites. His humility in the first act of the play is more than half real. The error in his portraiture is not the extravagant hocus-pocus of supposed Indian necromancers by which he is so easily duped, but the premature disclosure of villainy in his temptation of the two apprentices of his brother. But for this, he would be a perfect chameleon of circumstance. Here, again, we feel that Massinger was conscious only of inventing a rascal of the old simpler farce type. But the play is not a farce, in the sense in which *The Jew of Malta, The Alchemist, Bartholomew Fair* are farces. Massinger had not the personality to create great farce, and he was too serious to invent trivial farce. The ability to perform that slight distortion of *all* the elements in the world of a play or a story, so that this world is complete in itself, which was given to Marlowe and Jonson (and to Rabelais) and which is prerequisite to great farce, was denied to Massinger. On the other hand, his temperament was more closely related to theirs than to that of Shirley or the Restoration wits. His two comedies therefore occupy a place by themselves. His ways of thinking and feeling isolate him from both the Elizabethan and the later Caroline mind. He might almost have been a great realist; he is killed by conventions which were suitable for the preceding literary generation, but not for his. Had Massinger been a greater man, a man of more intellectual courage, the current of English literature immediately after him might have taken a different course. The defect is precisely a defect of personality. He is not, however, the only man of letters who, at the moment when a new view of life is wanted, has looked at life through the eyes of his predecessors, and only at manners through his own.

# SWINBURNE AS POET

IT is a question of some nicety to decide how much must be read of any particular poet. And it is not a question merely of the size of the poet. There are some poets whose every line has unique value. There are others who can be taken by a few poems universally agreed upon. There are others who need be read only in selections, but what selections are read will not very much matter. Of Swinburne, we should like to have the *Atalanta* entire, and a volume of selections which should certainly contain *The Leper, Laus Veneris,* and *The Triumph of Time.* It ought to contain many more, but there is perhaps no other single poem which it would be an error to omit. A student of Swinburne will want to read one of the Stuart plays and dip into *Tristram of Lyonesse.* But almost no one, to-day, will wish to read the whole of Swinburne. It is not because Swinburne is voluminous; certain poets, equally voluminous, must be read entire. The necessity and the difficulty of a selection are due to the peculiar nature of Swinburne's contribution, which, it is hardly too much to say, is of a very different kind from that of any other poet of equal reputation.

We may take it as undisputed that Swinburne did make a contribution; that he did something that had not been done before, and that what he did will not turn out to be a fraud. And from that we may proceed to inquire what Swinburne's contribution was, and why, whatever critical solvents we employ to break down the structure of his verse, this contribution remains. The test is this: agreed that we do not (and I think that the present generation does not) greatly enjoy Swinburne, and agreed that (a more serious condemnation) at one period of our lives we did enjoy him and now no longer enjoy him; nevertheless, the words which we use to state our grounds of dislike or indifference cannot be applied to Swinburne as they can to bad poetry. The words of condemnation are words which express his qualities. You may say "diffuse." But the diffuseness is essential; had Swinburne practised greater concentration his verse would be, not better in the same kind, but a different thing. His diffuseness is one of his glories. That so little material as appears to be employed in

*The Triumph of Time* should release such an amazing number of words, requires what there is no reason to call anything but genius. You could not condense *The Triumph of Time*. You could only leave out. And this would destroy the poem; though no one stanza seems essential. Similarly, a considerable quantity—a volume of selections—is necessary to give the quality of Swinburne although there is perhaps no one poem essential in this selection.

If, then, we must be very careful in applying terms of censure, like "diffuse," we must be equally careful of praise. "The beauty of Swinburne's verse is the sound," people say, explaining, "he had little visual imagination." I am inclined to think that the word "beauty" is hardly to be used in connection with Swinburne's verse at all; but in any case the beauty or effect of sound is neither that of music nor that of poetry which can be set to music. There is no reason why verse intended to be sung should not present a sharp visual image or convey an important intellectual meaning, for it supplements the music by another means of affecting the feelings. What we get in Swinburne is an expression by sound, which could not possibly associate itself with music. For what he gives is not images and ideas and music, it is one thing with a curious mixture of suggestions of all three.

> Shall I come, if I swim? wide are the waves, you see;
> Shall I come, if I fly, my dear Love, to thee?

This is Campion, and an example of the kind of music that is not to be found in Swinburne. It is an arrangement and choice of words which has a sound-value and at the same time a coherent comprehensible meaning, and the two things—the musical value and meaning—are two things, not one. But in Swinburne, there is no *pure* beauty—no pure beauty of sound, or of image, or of idea.

> Music, when soft voices die,
> Vibrates in the memory;
> Odours, when sweet violets sicken,
> Live within the sense they quicken.
>
> Rose leaves, when the rose is dead,
> Are heaped for the beloved's bed;
> And so thy thoughts, when thou art gone,
> Love itself shall slumber on.

I quote from Shelley, because Shelley is supposed to be the master of
Swinburne; and because his song, like that of Campion, has what
Swinburne has not—a beauty of music and a beauty of content; and
because it is clearly and simply expressed, with only two adjectives. Now,
in Swinburne the meaning and the sound are one thing. He is concerned
with the meaning of the word in a peculiar way: he employs, or rather
"works," the word's meaning. And this is connected with an interesting
fact about his vocabulary: he uses the most general word, because his
emotion is never particular, never in direct line of vision, never focused;
it is emotion reinforced, not by intensification, but by expansion.

> There lived a singer in France of old
> By the tideless dolorous midland sea.
> In a land of sand and ruin and gold
> There shone one woman, and none but she.

You see that Provence is the merest point of diffusion here. Swinburne
defines the place by the most general word, which has for him its own
value. "Gold," "ruin," "dolorous": it is not merely the sound that he wants,
but the vague associations of idea that the words give him. He has not his
eye on a particular place, as

> Li ruscelletti che dei verdi colli
> Del Casentin discendon giuso in Arno . . .

It is, in fact, the word that gives him the thrill, not the object. When you
take to pieces any verse of Swinburne, you find always that the object was
not there—only the word. Compare

> Snowdrops that plead for pardon
> And pine for fright

with the daffodils that come before the swallow dares. The snowdrop of
Swinburne disappears, the daffodil of Shakespeare remains. The swallow
of Shakespeare remain in the verse in *Macbeth*; the bird of Wordsworth

> Breaking the silence of the seas

remains; the swallow of "Itylus" disappears. Compare, again, a chorus of
*Atalanta* with a chorus from Athenian tragedy. The chorus of Swinburne
is almost a parody of the Athenian: it is sententious, but it has not even
the significance of commonplace.

At least we witness of thee ere we die
That these things are not otherwise, but thus. . . .

Before the beginning of years
    There came to the making of man
Time with a gift of tears;
    Grief with a glass that ran. . . .

This is not merely "music"; it is effective because it appears to be a tremendous statement, like statements made in our dreams; when we wake up we find that the "glass that ran" would do better for time than for grief, and that the gift of tears would be as appropriately bestowed by grief as by time.

It might seem to be intimated, by what has been said, that the work of Swinburne can be shown to be a sham, just as bad verse is a sham. It would only be so if you could produce or suggest something that it pretends to be and is not. The world of Swinburne does not depend upon some other world which it simulates; it has the necessary completeness and self-sufficiency for justification and permanence. It is impersonal, and no one else could have made it. The deductions are true to the postulates. It is indestructible. None of the obvious complaints that were or might have been brought to bear upon the first *Poems and Ballads* holds good. The poetry is not morbid, it is not erotic, it is not destructive. These are adjectives which can be applied to the material, the human feelings, which in Swinburne's case do not exist. The morbidity is not of human feeling but of language. Language in a healthy state presents the object, is so close to the object that the two are identified.

They are identified in the verse of Swinburne solely because the object has ceased to exist, because the meaning is merely the hallucination of meaning, because language, uprooted, has adapted itself to an independent life of atmospheric nourishment. In Swinburne, for example, we see the word "weary" flourishing in this way independent of the particular and actual weariness of flesh or spirit. The bad poet dwells partly in a world of objects and partly in a world of words, and he never can get them to fit. Only a man of genius could dwell so exclusively and consistently among words as Swinburne. His language is not, like the language of bad poetry, dead. It is very much alive, with this singular life of its own. But the language which is more important to us is that which is struggling to digest and express new objects, new groups of objects, new feelings, new aspects, as, for instance, the prose of Mr. James Joyce or the earlier Conrad.

# BLAKE

## I

IF one follow Blake's mind through the several stages of his poetic development it is impossible to regard him as a naïf, a wild man, a wild pet for the supercultivated. The strangeness is evaporated, the peculiarity is seen to be the peculiarity of all great poetry: something which is found (not everywhere) in Homer and Æschylus and Dante and Villon, and profound and concealed in the work of Shakespeare—and also in another form in Montaigne and in Spinoza. It is merely a peculiar honesty, which, in a world too frightened to be honest, is peculiarly terrifying. It is an honesty against which the whole world conspires, because it is unpleasant. Blake's poetry has the unpleasantness of great poetry. Nothing that can be called morbid or abnormal or perverse, none of the things which exemplify the sickness of an epoch or a fashion, have this quality; only those things which, by some extraordinary labour of simplification, exhibit the essential sickness or strength of the human soul. And this honesty never exists without great technical accomplishment. The question about Blake the man is the question of the circumstances that concurred to permit this honesty in his work, and what circumstances define its limitations. The favouring conditions probably include these two: that, being early apprenticed to a manual occupation, he was not compelled to acquire any other education in literature than he wanted, or to acquire it for any other reason than that he wanted it; and that, being a humble engraver, he had no journalistic-social career open to him.

There was, that is to say, nothing to distract him from his interests or to corrupt these interests: neither the ambitions of parents or wife, nor the standards of society, nor the temptations of success; nor was he exposed to imitation of himself or of anyone else. These circumstances—not his supposed inspired and untaught spontaneity—are what make him innocent. His early poems show what the poems of a boy of genius ought to show, immense power of assimilation. Such early poems are not, as usually supposed, crude attempts to do something beyond the boy's capacity; they are, in the case of a boy of real promise, more likely to be quite mature and successful attempts to do something small. So with Blake, his early poems are technically admirable, and their originality is in an occasional rhythm. The verse of *Edward III* deserves study. But his affection for certain Elizabethans is not so surprising as his affinity with the very best work of his own century. He is very like Collins, he is very eighteenth century. The poem *Whether on Ida's shady brow* is eighteenth-century work; the movement, the weight of it, the syntax, the choice of words—

> The *languid* strings do scarcely move!
> The sound is *forc'd*, the notes are few!

this is contemporary with Gray and Collins, it is the poetry of a language which has undergone the discipline of prose. Blake up to twenty is decidedly a traditional.

Blake's beginnings as a poet, then, are as normal as the beginnings of Shakespeare. His method of composition, in his mature work, is exactly like that of other poets. He has an idea (a feeling, an image), he develops it by accretion or expansion, alters his verse often, and hesitates often over the final choice.[1] The idea, of course, simply comes, but upon arrival it is subjected to prolonged manipulation. In the first phase Blake is concerned with verbal beauty; in the second he becomes the apparent naïf, really the mature intelligence. It is only when the ideas become more automatic, come more freely and are less manipulated, that we begin to suspect their origin, to suspect that they spring from a shallower source.

The Songs of Innocence and of Experience, and the poems from the Rossetti manuscript, are the poems of a man with a profound interest in human emotions, and a profound knowledge of them. The emotions are presented in an extremely simplified, abstract form. This form is one illustration of the external struggle of art against education, of the literary artist against the continuous deterioration of language.

---

[1] I do not know why M. Berger should say, without qualification, in his *William Blake: mysticisme et poésie,* that "son respect pour l'esprit qui soufflait en lui et qui dictait ses paroles l'empêchait de les corriger jamais." Dr. Sampson, in his Oxford edition of Blake, gives us to understand that Blake believed much of his writing to be automatic, but observes that Blake's "meticulous care in composition is everywhere apparent in the poems preserved in rough draft . . . alteration on alteration, rearrangement after rearrangement, deletions, additions, and inversions. . . ."

It is important that the artist should be highly educated in his own art; but his education is one that is hindered rather than helped by the ordinary processes of society which constitute education for the ordinary man. For these processes consist largely in the acquisition of impersonal ideas which obscure what we really are and feel, what we really want, and what really excites our interest. It is of course not the actual information acquired, but the conformity which the accumulation of knowledge is apt to impose, that is harmful. Tennyson is a very fair example of a poet almost wholly encrusted with parasitic opinion, almost wholly merged into his environment. Blake, on the other hand, knew what interested him, and he therefore presents only the essential, only, in fact, what can be presented, and need not be explained. And because he was not distracted, or frightened, or occupied in anything but exact statement, he understood. He was naked, and saw man naked, and from the centre of his own crystal. To him there was no more reason why Swedenborg should be absurd than Locke. He accepted Swedenborg, and eventually rejected him, for reasons of his own. He approached everything with a mind unclouded by current opinions. There was nothing of the superior person about him. This makes him terrifying.

## II

But if there was nothing to distract him from sincerity there were, on the other hand, the dangers to which the naked man is exposed. His philosophy, like his visions, like his insight, like his technique, was his own. And accordingly he was inclined to attach more importance to it than an artist should; this is what makes him eccentric, and makes him inclined to formlessness.

> But most through midnight streets I hear
> How the youthful harlot's curse
> Blasts the new-born infant's tear,
> And blights with plagues the marriage hearse,

is the naked vision;

> Love seeketh only self to please,
> To bind another to its delight,
> Joys in another's loss of ease,
> And builds a Hell in Heaven's despite,

is the naked observation; and *The Marriage of Heaven and Hell* is naked philosophy, presented. But Blake's occasional marriages of poetry and philosophy are not so felicitous.

> He who would do good to another must do it in Minute Particulars
> General Good is the plea of the scoundrel, hypocrite, and flatterer;
> For Art and Science cannot exist but in minutely organized particulars. . . .

One feels that the form is not well chosen. The borrowed philosophy of Dante and Lucretius is perhaps not so interesting, but it injures their form less. Blake did not have that more Mediterranean gift of form which knows how to borrow as Dante borrowed his theory of the soul; he must needs create a philosophy as well as a poetry. A similar formlessness attacks his draughtsmanship. The fault is most evident, of course, in the longer poems—or rather, the poems in which structure is important. You cannot create a very large poem without introducing a more impersonal point of view, or splitting it up into various personalities. But the weakness of the long poems is certainly not that they are too visionary, too remote from the world. It is that Blake did not see enough, became too much occupied with ideas.

We have the same respect for Blake's philosophy (and perhaps for that of Samuel Butler) that we have for an ingenious piece of home-made furniture: we admire the man who has put it together out of the odds and ends about the house. England has produced a fair number of these resourceful Robinson Crusoes; but we are not really so remote from the Continent, or from our own past, as to be deprived of the advantages of culture if we wish them.

We may speculate, for amusement, whether it would not have been beneficial to the north of Europe generally, and to Britain in particular, to have had a more continuous religious history. The local divinities of Italy were not wholly exterminated by Christianity, and they were not reduced to the dwarfish fate which fell upon our trolls and pixies. The latter, with the major Saxon deities, were perhaps no great loss in themselves, but they left an empty place; and perhaps our mythology was further impoverished by the divorce from Rome. Milton's celestial and infernal regions are large but insufficiently furnished apartments filled by heavy conversation; and one remarks about the Puritan mythology an historical thinness. And about Blake's supernatural territories, as about the supposed ideas that dwell there, we cannot help commenting on a certain meanness of culture. They illustrate the crankiness, the eccentricity, which frequently affects writers outside of the Latin traditions, and which such a critic as Arnold should certainly have rebuked. And they are not essential to Blake's inspiration.

Blake was endowed with a capacity for considerable understanding of human nature, with a remarkable and original sense of language and the music of language, and a gift of hallucinated vision. Had these been controlled by a respect for impersonal reason, for common sense, for the objectivity of science, it would have been better for him. What his genius required, and what it sadly lacked, was a framework of accepted and traditional ideas which would have prevented him from indulging in a philosophy of his own, and concentrated his attention upon the problems of the poet. Confusion of thought, emotion, and vision is what we find in such a work as *Also Sprach Zarathustra;* it is eminently not a Latin virtue. The concentration resulting from a framework of mythology and theology and philosophy is one of the reasons why Dante is a classic, and Blake only a poet of genius. The fault is perhaps not with Blake himself, but with the environment which failed to provide what such a poet needed; perhaps the circumstances compelled him to fabricate, perhaps the poet required the philosopher and mythologist; although the conscious Blake may have been quite unconscious of the motives.

# DANTE

M. Paul Valéry, a writer for whom I have considerable respect, has placed in his most recent statement upon poetry a paragraph which seems to me of very doubtful validity. I have not seen the complete essay, and know the quotation only as it appears in a critical notice in the *Athenæum,* July 23, 1920:

> La philosophie, et même la morale tendirent à fuir les œuvres pour se placer dans les réflexions qui les précèdent.... Parler aujourd'hui de poésie philosophique (fût-ce en invoquant Alfred de Vigny, Leconte de Lisle, et quelques autres), c'est naïvement confondre des conditions et des applications de l'esprit incompatibles entre elles. N'est-ce pas oublier que le but de celui qui spécule est de fixer ou de créer une notion—c'est-à-dire un *pouvoir* et un *instrument de pouvoir,* cependant que le poète moderne essaie de produire en nous un *état* et de porter cet état exceptionnel au point d'une jouissance parfaite....

It may be that I do M. Valéry an injustice which I must endeavour to repair when I have the pleasure of reading his article entire. But the paragraph gives the impression of more than one error of analysis. In the first place, it suggests that conditions have changed, that "philosophical" poetry may once have been permissible, but that (perhaps owing to the greater specialization of the modern world) it is now intolerable. We are forced to assume that what we do not like in our time was never good art, and that what appears to us good was always so. If any ancient "philosophical" poetry retains its value, a value which we fail to find in modern poetry of the same type, we investigate on the assumption that we shall find some difference to which the mere difference of date is irrelevant. But if it be maintained that the older poetry has a "philosophic" element and a "poetic" element which can be isolated, we have two tasks to perform. We must show first in a particular case—our case is Dante—that the philosophy is essential to the structure and that the structure is essential to the poetic beauty of the parts; and we must show that the philosophy

93

is employed in a different form from that which it takes in admittedly unsuccessful philosophical poems. And if M. Valéry is in error in his complete exorcism of "philosophy," perhaps the basis of the error is his apparently commendatory interpretation of the effort of the modern poet, namely, that the latter endeavours "to produce in us a *state*."

The early philosophical poets, Parmenides and Empedocles, were apparently persons of an impure philosophical inspiration. Neither their predecessors nor their successors expressed themselves in verse; Parmenides and Empedocles were persons who mingled with genuine philosophical ability a good deal of the emotion of the founder of a second-rate religious system. They were not interested exclusively in philosophy, or religion, or poetry, but in something which was a mixture of all three; hence their reputation as poets is low and as philosophers should be considerably below Heraclitus, Zeno, Anaxagoras, or Democritus. The poem of Lucretius is quite a different matter. For Lucretius was undoubtedly a poet. He endeavours to expound a philosophical system, but with a different motive from Parmenides or Empedocles, for this system is already in existence; he is really endeavouring to find the concrete poetic equivalent for this system—to find its complete equivalent in vision. Only, as he is an innovator in this art, he wavers between philosophical poetry and philosophy. So we find passages such as:

> But the velocity of thunderbolts is great and their stroke powerful, and they run through their course with a rapid descent, because the force when aroused first in all cases collects itself in the clouds and . . . Let us now sing what causes the motion of the stars. . . . Of all these different smells then which strike the nostrils one may reach to a much greater distance than another. . . .[1]

But Lucretius' true tendency is to express an ordered vision of the life of man, with great vigour of real poetic image and often acute observation.

> quod petiere, premunt arte faciuntque dolorem
> corporis et dentes inlidunt saepe labellis
> osculaque adfligunt, quia non est pura voluptas
> et stimuli subsunt qui instigant laedere id ipsum
> quodcumque est, rabies unde illaec germina surgunt . . .
>
>          medio de fonte leporum
> surgit amari aliquid quod in ipsis floribus angat . . .

---

[1] Munro's translation, *passim.*

nec procumbere humi prostratum et pandere palmas
ante deum delubra nec aras sanguine multo
spargere quadrupedum nec votis nectere vota,
sed mage pacata posse omnia mente tueri.

The philosophy which Lucretius tackled was not rich enough in variety of feeling, applied itself to life too uniformly, to supply the material for a wholly successful poem. It was incapable of complete expansion into pure vision. But I must ask M. Valéry whether the "aim" of Lucretius' poem was "to fix or create a notion" or to fashion "an instrument of power."

Without doubt, the effort of the philosopher proper, the man who is trying to deal with ideas in themselves, and the effort of the poet, who may be trying to *realize* ideas, cannot be carried on at the same time. But this is not to deny that poetry can be in some sense philosophic. The poet can deal with philosophic ideas, not as matter for argument, but as matter for inspection. The original form of a philosophy cannot be poetic. But poetry can be penetrated by a philosophic idea, it can deal with this idea when it has reached the point of immediate acceptance, when it has become almost a physical modification. If we divorced poetry and philosophy altogether, we should bring a serious impeachment, not only against Dante, but against most of Dante's contemporaries.

Dante had the benefit of a mythology and a theology which had undergone a more complete absorption into life than those of Lucretius. It is curious that not only Dante's detractors, like the Petrarch of Landor's *Pentameron* (if we may apply so strong a word to so amiable a character), but some of his admirers, insist on the separation of Dante's "poetry" and Dante's "teaching." Sometimes the philosophy is confused with the allegory. The philosophy is an ingredient, it is a part of Dante's world just as it is a part of life; the allegory is the scaffold on which the poem is built. An American writer of a little primer of Dante, Mr. Henry Dwight Sidgwick, who desires to improve our understanding of Dante as a "spiritual leader," says:

> To Dante this literal Hell was a secondary matter; so it is to us. He and we are concerned with the allegory. That allegory is simple. Hell is the absence of God. . . . If the reader begins with the consciousness that he is reading about sin, spiritually understood, he never loses the thread, he is never at a loss, never slips back into the literal signification.

Without stopping to question Mr. Sidgwick on the difference between literal and spiritual sin, we may affirm that his remarks are misleading.

Undoubtedly the allegory is to be taken seriously, and certainly the *Comedy* is in some way a "moral education." The question is to find a formula for the correspondence between the former and the latter, to decide whether the moral value corresponds directly to the allegory. We can easily ascertain what importance Dante assigned to allegorical method. In the *Convivio* we are serious informed that

> the principal design [of the odes] is to lead men to knowledge and virtue, as will be seen in the progress of the truth of them;

and we are also given the familiar four interpretations of an ode: literal, allegorical, moral, and anagogical. And so distinguished a scholar as M. Hauvette repeats again and again the phrase "didactique d'intention." We accept the allegory. Accepted, there are two usual ways of dealing with it. One may, with Mr. Sidgwick, dwell upon its significance for the seeker of "spiritual light," or one may, with Landor, deplore the spiritual mechanics and find the poet only in passages where he frees himself from his divine purposes. With neither of these points of view can we concur. Mr. Sidgwick magnifies the "preacher and prophet," and presents Dante as a superior Isaiah or Carlyle; Landor reserves the poet, reprehends the scheme, and denounces the politics. Some of Landor's errors are more palpable than Mr. Sidgwick's. He errs, in the first place, in judging Dante by the standards of classical epic. Whatever the *Comedy* is, an epic it is not. M. Hauvette well says:

> Rechercher dans quelle mesure le poème se rapproche du genre classique de l'épopée, et dans quelle mesure il s'en écarte, est un exércice de rhétorique entièrement inutile, puisque Dante, à n'en pas douter, n'a jamais eu l'intention de composer une action épique dans les règles.

But we must define the framework of Dante's poem from the result as well as from the intention. The poem has not only a framework, but a form; and even if the framework be allegorical, the form may be something else. The examination of any episode in the *Comedy* ought to show that not merely the allegorical interpretation or the didactic intention, but the emotional significance itself, cannot be isolated from the rest of the poem. Landor appears, for instance, to have misunderstood such a passage as the Paolo and Francesca, by failing to perceive its relations:

> In the midst of her punishment, Francesca, when she comes to the
> tenderest part of her story, tells it with complacency and delight.

This is surely a false simplification. To have lost all recollected delight
would have been, for Francesca, either loss of humanity or relief from
damnation. The ecstasy, with the present thrill at the remembrance of it,
is a part of the torture. Francesca is neither stupefied nor reformed; she
is merely damned; and it is a part of damnation to experience desires that
we can no longer gratify. For in Dante's Hell souls are not deadened, as
they mostly are in life; they are actually in the greatest torment of which
each is capable.

> E il modo ancor m'offende.

It is curious that Mr. Sidgwick, whose approbation is at the opposite
pole from Landor's, should have fallen into a similar error. He says:

> In meeting [Ulysses], as in meeting Pier della Vigna and Brunetto
> Latini, the preacher and the prophet are lost in the poet.

Here, again, is a false simplification. These passages have no digressive
beauty. The case of Brunetto is parallel to that of Francesca. The emotion of the passage resides in Brunetto's excellence in damnation—so
admirable a soul, and so perverse.

> e parve de costoro
> Quegli che vince e non colui che perde.

And I think that if Mr. Sidgwick had pondered the strange words of
Ulysses,

> com' altrui piacque,

he would not have said that the preacher and prophet are lost in the poet.
"Preacher" and "prophet" are odious terms; but what Mr. Sidgwick des-
ignates by them is something which is certainly not "lost in the poet," but
is part of the poet.
  A variety of passages might illustrate the assertion that no emotion
is contemplated by Dante purely in and for itself. The emotion of the
person, or the emotion with which our attitude appropriately invests the

person, is never lost or diminished, is always preserved entire, but is modified by the position assigned to the person in the eternal scheme, is
coloured by the atmosphere of that person's residence in one of the three
worlds. About none of Dante's characters is there that ambiguity which
affects Milton's Lucifer. The damned preserve any degree of beauty or
grandeur that ever rightly pertained to them, and this intensifies and also
justifies their damnation. As Jason

> Guarda quel grande che viene!
> E per dolor non par lagrima spanda,
> Quanto aspetto reale ancor ritiene!

The crime of Bertrand becomes more lurid; the vindictive Adamo
acquires greater ferocity, and the errors of Arnaut are corrected—

> Poi s'ascose nel foco che gli affina.

If the artistic emotion presented by any episode of the *Comedy* is
dependent upon the whole, we may proceed to inquire what the whole
scheme is. The usefulness of allegory and astronomy is obvious. A
mechanical framework, in a poem of so vast an ambit, was a necessity. As
the centre of gravity of emotions is more remote from a single human
action, or a system of purely human actions, than in drama or epic, so the
framework has to be more artificial and apparently more mechanical. It is
not essential that the allegory or the almost unintelligible astronomy
should be understood—only that its presence should be justified. The
emotional structure within this scaffold is what must be understood—the
structure made possible by the scaffold. This structure is an ordered scale
of human emotions. Not, necessarily, *all* human emotions; and in any case
all the emotions are limited, and also extended in significance by their
place in the scheme.

But Dante's is the most comprehensive, and the most *ordered* presentation of emotions that has ever been made. Dante's method of dealing with
any emotion may be contrasted, not so appositely with that of other
"epic" poets as with that of Shakespeare. Shakespeare takes a character
apparently controlled by a simple emotion, and analyses the character
and the emotion itself. The emotion is split up into constituents—and
perhaps destroyed in the process. The mind of Shakespeare was one of
the most *critical* that has ever existed. Dante, on the other hand, does not
analyse the emotion so much as he exhibits its relation to the other emotions. You cannot, that is, understand the *Inferno* without the *Purgatorio*

and the *Paradiso*. "Dante," says Landor's Petrarch, "is the great master of the disgusting." That is true, though Sophocles at least once approaches him. But a disgust like Dante's is no hypertrophy of a single reaction: it is completed and explained only by the last canto of the Paradiso.

> La forma universal di questo nodo
> credo ch'io vidi, perchè più di largo
> dicendo questo, mi sento ch'io godo.

The contemplation of the horrid or sordid or disgusting, by an artist, is the necessary and negative aspect of the impulse toward the pursuit of beauty. But not all succeed as did Dante in expressing the complete scale from negative to positive. The negative is the more importunate.

The structure of emotions, for which the allegory is the necessary scaffold, is complete from the most sensuous to the most intellectual and the most spiritual. Dante gives a concrete presentation of the most elusive:

> Pareva a me che nube ne coprisse
> lucida, spessa, solida e polita,
> quasi adamante che lo sol ferisse.
>
> Per entro sè l'eterna margarita
> ne recepette, com' acqua recepe
> raggio di luce, permanendo unita.

or

> Nel suo aspetto tal dentro mi fei,
> qual si fe' Glauco nel gustar dell' erba,
> che il fe' consorto in mar degli altri dei.[1]

Again, in the *Purgatorio*, for instance in Canto XVI and Canto XVIII, occur passages of pure exposition of philosophy, the philosophy of Aristotle strained through the schools.

> Lo natural e sempre senza errore,
> ma l' altro puote errar per malo obbietto,
> o per poco o per troppo di vigore . . .

---

[1] See E. Pound, *The Spirit of Romance*, p. 145.

We are not here studying the philosophy, we *see* it, as part of the ordered world. The aim of the poet is to state a vision, and no vision of life can be complete which does not include the articulate formulation of life which human minds make.

> Onde convenne legge per fren porre . . .

It is one of the greatest merits of Dante's poem that the vision is so nearly complete; it is evidence of this greatness that the significance of any single passage, of any of the passages that are selected as "poetry," is incomplete unless we ourselves apprehend the whole.

And Dante helps us to provide a criticism of M. Valéry's "modern poet" who attempts "to produce in us a *state*." A state, in itself, is nothing whatever.

M. Valéry's account is quite in harmony with pragmatic doctrine, and with the tendencies of such a work as William James's *Varieties of Religious Experience*. The mystical experience is supposed to be valuable because it is a pleasant state of unique intensity. But the true mystic is not satisfied merely by feeling, he must pretend at least that he *sees*, and the absorption into the divine is only the necessary, if paradoxical, limit of this contemplation. The poet does not aim to excite—that is not even a test of his success—but to set something down; the state of the reader is merely that reader's particular mode of perceiving what the poet has caught in words. Dante, more than any other poet, has succeeded in dealing with his philosophy, not as a theory (in the modern and not the Greek sense of that word) or as his own comment or reflection, but in terms of something *perceived*. When most of our modern poets confine themselves to what they had perceived, they produce for us, usually, only odds and ends of still life and stage properties; but that does not imply so much that the method of Dante is obsolete, as that our vision is perhaps comparatively restricted.

NOTE.—My friend the Abbé Laban has reproached me for attributing to Landor, in this essay, sentiments which are merely the expression of his dramatic figure Petrarch, and which imply rather Landor's reproof of the limitations of the historical Petrarch's view of Dante, than the view of Landor himself. The reader should therefore observe this correction of my use of Landor's honoured name.

# ANDREW MARVELL

THE tercentenary of the former member for Hull deserves not only the celebration proposed by that favoured borough, but a little serious reflection upon his writing. That is an act of piety, which is very different from the resurrection of a deceased reputation. Marvell has stood high for some years; his best poems are not very many, and not only must be well known, from the "Golden Treasury" and the "Oxford Book of English Verse," but must also have been enjoyed by numerous readers. His grave needs neither rose nor rue nor laurel; there is no imaginary justice to be done; we may think about him, if there be need for thinking, for our own benefit, not his. To bring the poet back to life—the great, the perennial, task of criticism—is in this case to squeeze the drops of the essence of two or three poems; even confining ourselves to these, we may find some precious liquor unknown to the present age. Not to determine rank, but to isolate this quality, is the critical labour. The fact that of all Marvell's verse, which is itself not a great quantity, the really valuable part consists of a very few poems indicates that the unknown quality of which we speak is probably a literary rather than a personal quality; or, more truly, that it is a quality of a civilization, of a traditional habit of life. A poet like Donne, or like Baudelaire or Laforgue, may almost be considered the inventor of an attitude, a system of feeling or of morals. Donne is difficult to analyse: what appears at one time a curious personal point of view may at another time appear rather the precise concentration of a kind of feeling diffused in the air about him. Donne and his shroud, the shroud and his motive for wearing it, are inseparable, but they are not the same thing. The seventeenth century sometimes seems for more than a moment to gather up and to digest into its art all the experience of the human mind which (from the same point of view) the later centuries seem to have been partly engaged in repudiating. But Donne would have been an individual at any time and place; Marvell's best verse is the product of European, that is to say Latin, culture.

Out of that high style developed from Marlowe through Jonson (for Shakespeare does not lend himself to these genealogies) the seventeenth century separated two qualities: wit and magniloquence. Neither is as simple or as apprehensible as its name seems to imply, and the two are not in practice antithetical; both are conscious and cultivated, and the mind which cultivates one may cultivate the other. The actual poetry, of Marvell, of Cowley, of Milton and of others, is a blend in varying proportions. And we must be on guard not to employ the terms with too wide a comprehension; for like the other fluid terms with which literary criticism deals, the meaning alters with the age, and for precision we must rely to some degree upon the literacy and good taste of the reader. The wit of the Caroline poets is not the wit of Shakespeare, and it is not the wit of Dryden, the great master of contempt, or of Pope, the great master of hatred, or of Swift, the great master of disgust. What is meant is something which is a common quality to the songs in *Comus* and Cowley's Anacreontics and Marvell's Horatian Ode. It is more than a technical accomplishment, or the vocabulary and syntax of an epoch; it is, what we have designated tentatively as wit, a tough reasonableness beneath the slight lyric grace. You cannot find it in Shelley or Keats or Wordsworth; you cannot find more than an echo of it in Landor; still less in Tennyson or Browning; and among contemporaries Mr. Yeats is an Irishman and Mr. Hardy is a modern Englishman—that is to say, Mr. Hardy is without it and Mr. Yeats is outside of the tradition altogether. On the other hand, as it certainly exists in Lafontaine, there is a large part of it in Gautier. And of the magniloquence, the deliberate exploitation of the possibilities of magnificence in language which Milton used and abused, there is also use and even abuse in the poetry of Baudelaire.

Wit is not a quality that we are accustomed to associate with "Puritan" literature, with Milton or with Marvell. But if so, we are at fault partly in our conception of wit and partly in our generalizations about the Puritans. And if the wit of Dryden or of Pope is not the only kind of wit in the language, the rest is not merely a little merriment or a little levity or a little impropriety or a little epigram. And, on the other hand, the sense in which a man like Marvell is a "Puritan" is restricted. The persons who opposed Charles I. and the persons who supported the Commonwealth were not all of the flock of Rabbi Zeal-of-the-land Busy or the United Grand Junction Ebenezer Temperance Association. Many of them were gentlemen of the time who merely believed, with considerable show of reason, that government by a Parliament of gentlemen was better than government by a Stuart; though they were, to that extent, Liberal

Practitioners, they could hardly foresee the tea-meeting and the Dissidence of Dissent. Being men of education and culture, even of travel, some of them were exposed to that spirit of the age which was coming to be the French spirit of the age. This spirit, curiously enough, was quite opposed to the tendencies latent or the forces active in Puritanism; the contest does great damage to the poetry of Milton; Marvell, an active servant of the public, but a lukewarm partisan, and a poet on a smaller scale, is far less injured by it. His line on the statue of Charles II., "It is such a King as no chisel can mend," may be set off against his criticism of the Great Rebellion: "Men . . . ought and might have trusted the King." Marvell, therefore, more a man of the century than a Puritan, speaks more clearly and unequivocally with the voice of his literary age than does Milton.

This voice speaks out uncommonly strong in the "Coy Mistress." The theme is one of the great traditional commonplaces of European literature. It is the theme of "O mistress mine," of "Gather ye rosebuds," of "Go, lovely rose"; it is in the savage austerity of Lucretius and the intense levity of Catullus. Where the wit of Marvell renews the theme is in the variety and order of the images. In the first of the three paragraphs Marvell plays with a fancy which begins by pleasing and leads to astonishment.

> Had we but world enough and time,
> This coyness, lady, were no crime,
>     . . . I would
> Love you ten years before the Flood,
> And you should, if you please, refuse
> Till the conversion of the Jews;
> My vegetable love should grow
> Vaster than empires and more slow. . . .

We notice the high speed, the succession of concentrated images, each magnifying the original fancy. When this process has been carried to the end and summed up, the poem turns suddenly with that surprise which has been one of the most important means of poetic effect since Homer:—

> But at my back I always hear
> Time's wingèd chariot hurrying near,
> And yonder all before us lie
> Deserts of vast eternity.

A whole civilization resides in these lines:—

> Pallida Mors aequa pulsat pede pauperum tabernas,
> Regumque turris. . . .
> Eheu fugaces, Postume, Postume,
> Labuntur anni. . . .
> Post equitem sedet atra, Cura.

And not only Horace but Catullus himself:—

> Nobis, cum semel occidit brevis lux,
> Nox est perpetua una dormienda.

The verse of Marvell has not the grand reverberation of Catullus's Latin; but the image of Marvell is certainly more comprehensive and penetrates greater depths than any of those quoted from Horace.

A modern poet, had he reached the height, would very likely have closed on this moral reflection. But the three strophes of Marvell's poem have something like a syllogistic relation to each other. After a close approach to the mood of Donne,

> then worms shall try
> That long-preserved virginity . . .
> The grave's a fine and private place,
> But none, I think, do there embrace,

the conclusion,

> Let us roll all our strength and all
> Our sweetness up into one ball,
> And tear our pleasures with rough strife,
> Thorough the iron gates of life.

It will hardly be denied that this poem contains wit; but it may not be evident that this wit forms the crescendo and diminuendo of a scale of great imaginative power. The wit is not only combined with, but fused into, the imagination. We can easily recognize a witty fancy in the successive images ("my *vegetable* love," "till the conversion of the Jews"), but this fancy is not indulged, as it sometimes is by Cowley or Cleveland, for its own sake. It is structural decoration of a serious idea. In this it is superior to the fancy of "L'Allegro," "Il Penseroso," or the lighter and less successful poems of Keats. In fact, this alliance of levity and seriousness (by which the seriousness is intensified) is a characteristic of the sort of wit we are trying to identify. It is found in

Le squelette était invisible
Au temps heureux de l'art païen!

of Gautier, and in the *dandyisme* of Baudelaire and Laforgue. It is in
the poem of Catullus which has been quoted, and in the variation by
Ben Jonson:—

> Cannot we deceive the eyes
> Of a few poor household spies?
> 'Tis no sin love's fruits to steal,
> But that sweet sin to reveal,
> To be taken, to be seen,
> These have sins accounted been.

It is in Propertius and Ovid. It is a quality of a sophisticated literature; a
quality which expands in English literature just at the moment before the
English mind altered; it is not a quality which we should expect Puritanism
to encourage. When we come to Gray and Collins, the sophistication
remains only in the language, and has disappeared from the feeling. Gray
and Collins were masters, but they had lost that hold on human values,
that firm grasp of human experience, which is a formidable achievement
of the Elizabethan and Jacobean poets. This wisdom, cynical perhaps but
untired (in Shakespeare, a terrifying clairvoyance) leads toward, and is
only completed by, the religious comprehension; it leads to the point of
the *Ainsi tout leur a craqué dans la main* of Bouvard and Pécuchet.

The difference between imagination and fancy, in view of this poetry
of wit, is a very narrow one. Obviously, an image which is immediately
and unintentionally ridiculous is merely a fancy. In the poem "Upon
Appleton House," Marvell falls in with one of these undesirable images,
describing the attitude of the house toward its master:—

> Yet thus the laden house does sweat,
> And scarce endures the master great;
> But, where he comes, the swelling hall
> Stirs, and the square grows spherical;

which, whatever its intention, is more absurd than it was intended to be.
Marvell also falls into the even commoner error of images which are
overdeveloped or distracting; which support nothing but their own mis-
shapen bodies:—

> And now the salmon-fishers moist
> Their leathern boats begin to hoist;
> And, like Antipodes in shoes,
> Have shod their heads in their canoes.

Of this sort of image a choice collection may be found in Johnson's "Life of Cowley." But the images in the "Coy Mistress" are not only witty, but satisfy the elucidation of Imagination given by Coleridge:—

> This power . . . reveals itself in the balance or reconcilement of opposite or discordant qualities: of sameness, with difference; of the general, with the concrete; the idea with the image; the individual with the representative; the sense of novelty and freshness with old and familiar objects; a more than usual state of emotion with more than usual order; judgment ever awake and steady self-possession with enthusiasm and feeling profound or vehement. . . .

Coleridge's statement applies also to the following verses, which are selected because of their similarity, and because they illustrate the marked caesura which Marvell often introduces in a short line:—

> The tawny mowers enter next,
> Who seem like Israelites to be
> Walking on foot through a green sea.

> And now the meadows fresher dyed,
> Whose grass, with moister colour dashed,
> Seems as green silks but newly washed.

> He hangs in shades the orange bright,
> Like golden lamps in a green night.

> Annihilating all that's made
> To a green thought in a green shade.

> Had it lived long, it would have been
> Lilies without, roses within.

The whole poem, from which the last of these quotations is drawn ("The Nymph and the Fawn"), is built upon a very slight foundation, and we can imagine what some of our modern practitioners of slight themes would have made of it. But we need not descend to an invidious contemporaneity to point the difference. Here are six lines from "The Nymph and the Fawn":—

> I have a garden of my own,
> But so with roses overgrown
> And lilies, that you would it guess
> To be a little wilderness;
> And all the spring-time of the year
> It only lovèd to be there.

And here are five lines from "The Nymph's Song to Hylas" in the "Life and Death of Jason," by William Morris:—

> I know a little garden close
> Set thick with lily and red rose.
> Where I would wander if I might
> From dewy dawn to dewy night,
> And have one with me wandering.

So far the resemblance is more striking than the difference, although we might just notice the vagueness of allusion in the last line to some indefinite person, form, or phantom, compared with the more explicit reference of emotion to object which we should expect from Marvell. But in the latter part of the poem Morris divaricates widely:—

> Yet tottering as I am, and weak,
> Still have I left a little breath
> To seek within the jaws of death
> An entrance to that happy place;
> To seek the unforgotten face
> Once seen, once kissed, once reft from me
> Anigh the murmuring of the sea.

Here the resemblance, if there is any, is to the latter part of "The Coy Mistress." As for the difference, it could not be more pronounced. The effect of Morris's charming poem depends upon the mistiness of the feeling and the vagueness of its object; the effect of Marvell's upon its bright, hard precision. And this precision is not due to the fact that Marvell is concerned with cruder or simpler or more carnal emotions. The emotion of Morris is not more refined or more spiritual; it is merely more vague: if anyone doubts whether the more refined or spiritual emotion can be

precise, he should study the treatment of the varieties of discarnate emotion in the "Paradiso." A curious result of the comparison of Morris's
poem with Marvell's is that the former, though it appears to be more
serious, is found to be the slighter; and Marvell's "Nymph and Fawn,"
appearing more slight, is the more serious.

> So weeps the wounded balsam; so
> The holy frankincense doth flow;
> The brotherless Heliades
> Melt in such amber tears as these.

Those verses have the suggestiveness of true poetry; and the verses of
Morris, which are nothing it not an attempt to suggest, really suggest
nothing; and we are inclined to infer that the suggestiveness is the aura
around a bright clear centre, that you cannot have the aura alone. The
day-dreamy feeling of Morris is essentially a slight thing; Marvell takes a
slight affair, the feeling of a girl for her pet, and gives it a connexion with
that inexhaustible and terrible nebula of emotion which surrounds all our
exact and practical passions and mingles with them. Again, Marvell does
this in a poem which, because of its formal pastoral machinery, may
appear a trifling object:—

> *Clorinda:*  Near this, a fountain's liquid bell
>              Tinkles within the concave shell.
>
> *Damon:*    Might a soul bathe there and be clean,
>             Or slake its drought?

where we find that a metaphor has suddenly rapt us to the image of spiritual purgation. There is here the element of *surprise*, as when Villon says:—

> Nécessité faict gens mesprendre
> Et faim saillir le loup des boys,

the surprise which Poe considered of the highest importance, and also the
restraint and quietness of tone which make the surprise possible. And in
the verses of Marvell which have been quoted there is the making the
familiar strange, and the strange familiar, which Coleridge attributed to
good poetry.

The effort to construct a dream-world, which alters English poetry
so greatly in the nineteenth century, a dream-world utterly different
from the visionary realities of the Vita Nuova or of the poetry of Dante's

contemporaries, is a problem of which various explanations may no
doubt be found; in any case, the result makes a poet of the nineteenth
century, of the same size as Marvell, a more trivial and less serious figure.
Marvell is no greater personality than William Morris, but he had something much more solid behind him: he had the vast and penetrating influence of Ben Jonson. Jonson never wrote anything so pure as Marvell's
Horatian Ode; but this ode has that same quality of wit which was diffused over the whole Elizabethan product and concentrated in the work
of Jonson. And, as was said before, this wit which pervades the poetry of
Marvell is more Latin, more refined, than anything that succeeded it. The
great danger, as well as the great interest and excitement, of English prose
and verse, compared with French, is that it permits and justifies an exag-
geration of particular qualities to the exclusion of others. Dryden was
great in wit, as Milton in magniloquence; but the former, by isolating this
quality and making it by itself into great poetry, and the latter, by coming to dispense with it altogether, may perhaps have injured the language.
In Dryden wit becomes almost fun, and thereby loses some contact with
reality; becomes pure fun, which French wit almost never is.

> The midwife placed her hand on his thick skull,
> With this prophetic blessing: *Be thou dull.*

> A numerous host of dreaming saints succeed,
> Of the true old enthusiastic breed.

This is audacious and splendid; it belongs to satire besides which Marvell's
Satires are random babbling; but it is perhaps as exaggerated as—

> Oft he seems to hide his face,
> But unexpectedly returns,
> And to his faithful champion hath in place
> Bore witness gloriously; whence Gaza mourns,
> And all that band them to resist
> His uncontrollable intent.

How oddly the sharp Dantesque phrase "whence Gaza mourns" springs
out from the brilliant but ridiculous contortions of Milton's sentence!

> Who from his private gardens, where
> He lived reserved and austere,
> (As if his highest plot
>     To plant the bergamot)

> Could by industrious valour climb
> To ruin the great work of Time,
> And cast the kingdoms old
>     Into another mold;
>         • • • •
> The Pict no shelter now shall find
> Within his parti-coloured mind,
> But, from this valour sad,
>     Shrink underneath the plaid:

There is an equipoise, a balance and proportion of tones, which, while it cannot raise Marvell to the level of Dryden or Milton, extorts an approval which these poets do not receive from us, and bestows a pleasure at least different in kind from any they can often give. It is what makes Marvell, in the best sense, a classic: classic in a sense in which Gray and Collins are not; for the latter, with all their accredited purity, are comparatively poor in shades of feeling to contrast and unite.

We are baffled in the attempt to translate the quality indicated by the dim and antiquated term wit into the equally unsatisfactory nomenclature of our own time. Even Cowley is only able to define it by negatives:—

> Comely in thousand shapes appears;
> Yonder we saw it plain; and here 'tis now,
> Like spirits in a place, we know not how.

It has passed out of our critical coinage altogether, and no new term has been struck to replace it; the quality seldom exists, and is never recognized.

> In a true piece of Wit all things must be
>     Yet all things there agree;
> As in the Ark, join'd without force or strife,
> All creatures dwelt, all creatures that had life.
>     Or as the primitive forms of all
>     (If we compare great things with small)
> Which, without discord or confusion, lie
> In that strange mirror of the Deity.

So far Cowley has spoken well. But if we are to attempt even no more than Cowley, we, placed in a retrospective attitude, must risk much more anxious generalizations. With our eye still on Marvell, we can say that wit is not erudition; it is sometimes stifled by erudition, as in much of Milton. It is not cynicism, though it has a kind of toughness which may be confused

with cynicism by the tender-minded. It is confused with erudition because
it belongs to an educated mind, rich in generations of experience; and it
is confused with cynicism because it implies a constant inspection and
criticism of experience. It involves, probably, a recognition, implicit in
the expression of every experience, of other kinds of experience which
are possible, which we find as clearly in the greatest as in poets like
Marvell. Such a general statement may seem to take us a long way from
"The Nymph and the Fawn," or even from the Horatian Ode; but it is
perhaps justified by the desire to account for that precise taste of
Marvell's which finds for him the proper degree of seriousness for every
subject which he treats. His errors of taste, when he trespasses, are not
sins against this virtue; they are conceits, distended metaphors and similes,
but they never consist in taking a subject too seriously or too lightly. This
virtue of wit is not a peculiar quality of minor poets, or of the minor
poets of one age or of one school; it is an intellectual quality which perhaps only becomes noticeable by itself, in the work of lesser poets.
Furthermore, it is absent from the work of Wordsworth, Shelley, and
Keats, on whose poetry nineteenth-century criticism has unconsciously
been based. To the best of their poetry wit is irrelevant:—

> Art thou pale for weariness
> Of climbing heaven and gazing on the earth,
> Wandering companionless
> Among the stars that have a different birth,
> And ever changing, like a joyless eye,
> That finds no object worth its constancy?

We should find it difficult to draw any useful comparison between these
lines of Shelley and anything by Marvell. But later poets, who would have
been the better for Marvell's quality, were without it; even Browning
seems oddly immature, in some way, beside Marvell. And nowadays we
find occasionally good irony, or satire, which lack wit's internal equilibri-
um, because their voices are essentially protests against some outside sen-
timentality or stupidity; or we find serious poets who are afraid of acquir-
ing wit, lest they lose intensity. The quality which Marvell had, this mod-
est and certainly impersonal virtue—whether we call it wit or reason, or
even urbanity—we have patently failed to define. By whatever name we
call it, and however we define that name, it is something precious and
needed and apparently extinct; it is what should preserve the reputation
of Marvel. C'était une belle ame, comme on ne fait plus à Londres.

# JOHN DRYDEN

IF the prospect of delight be wanting (which alone justifies the perusal of poetry) we may let the reputation of Dryden sleep in the manuals of literature. To those who are genuinely insensible of his genius (and these are probably the majority of living readers of poetry) we can only oppose illustrations of the following proposition: that their insensibility does not merely signify indifference to satire and wit, but lack of perception of qualities not confined to satire and wit and present in the work of other poets whom these persons feel that they understand. To those whose taste in poetry is formed entirely upon the English poetry of the nineteenth century—to the majority—it is difficult to explain or excuse Dryden: the twentieth century is still the nineteenth, although it may in time acquire its own character. The nineteenth century had, like every other, limited tastes and peculiar fashions; and, like every other, it was unaware of its own limitations. Its tastes and fashions had no place for Dryden; yet Dryden is one of the tests of a catholic appreciation of poetry.

He is a successor of Jonson, and therefore the descendant of Marlowe; he is the ancestor of nearly all that is best in the poetry of the eighteenth century. Once we have mastered Dryden—and by mastery is meant a full and essential enjoyment, not the enjoyment of a private whimsical fashion—we can extract whatever enjoyment and edification there is in his contemporaries—Oldham, Denham, or the less remunerative Waller; and still more his successors—not only Pope, but Phillips, Churchill, Gray, Johnson, Cowper, Goldsmith. His inspiration is prolonged in Crabbe and Byron; it even extends, as Mr. van Doren cleverly points out, to Poe. Even the poets responsible for the revolt were well acquainted with him: Wordsworth knew his work, and Keats invoked his aid. We cannot fully enjoy or rightly estimate a hundred years of English poetry unless we fully enjoy Dryden; and to enjoy Dryden means to pass beyond the limitations of the nineteenth century into a new freedom.

All, all of a piece throughout:
Thy Chase had a Beast in View;
Thy Wars brought nothing about;
Thy Lovers were all untrue.
'Tis well an Old Age is out,
And time to begin a New.
 . . . .
The world's great age begins anew,
The golden years return,
The earth doth like a snake renew
Her winter weeds outworn:
Heaven smiles, and faiths and empires gleam
Like wrecks of a dissolving dream.

The first of these passages is by Dryden, the second by Shelley; the second is found in the "Oxford Book of English Verse," the first is not; yet we might defy anyone to show that the second is superior on intrinsically poetic merit. It is easy to see why the second should appeal more readily to the nineteenth, and what is left of the nineteenth under the name of the twentieth, century. It is not so easy to see propriety in an image which divests a snake of "winter weeds"; and this is a sort of blemish which would have been noticed more quickly by a contemporary of Dryden than by a contemporary of Shelley.

These reflections are occasioned by an admirable book on Dryden which has appeared at this very turn of time, when taste is becoming perhaps more fluid and ready for a new mould.[1] It is a book which every practitioner of English verse should study. The consideration is so thorough, the matter so compact, the appreciation so just, temperate and enthusiastic, and supplied with such copious and well-chosen extracts from the poetry, the suggestion of astutely placed facts leads our thought so far, that there only remain to mention, as defects which do not detract from its value, two omissions: the prose is not dealt with, and the plays are somewhat slighted. What is especially impressive is the exhibition of the very wide range of Dryden's work, shown by the quotations of every species. Everyone knows "MacFlecknoe," and parts of "Absalom and Achitophel"; in consequence, Dryden has sunk by the persons he has elevated to distinction—Shadwell and Settle, Shaftesbury and Buckingham. Dryden was much more than a satirist; to dispose of him as a satirist is to

[1] *John Dryden*, by Mark van Doren (New York: Harcourt, Brace & Howe).

place an obstacle in the way of our understanding. At all events, we must satisfy ourselves of our definition of the term satire; we must not allow our familiarity with the word to blind us to differences and refinements; we must not assume that satire is a fixed type, and fixed to the prosaic, suited only to prose; we must acknowledge that satire is not the same thing in the hands of two different writers of genius. The connotations of "satire" and of "wit," in short, may be only prejudices of nineteenth-century taste. Perhaps, we think, after reading Mr. van Doren's book, a juster view of Dryden may be given by beginning with some other portion of his work than his celebrated satires; but even here there is much more present, and much more that is poetry, than is usually supposed.

The piece of Dryden's which is the most fun, which is the most sustained display of surprise after surprise of wit from line to line, is "MacFlecknoe." Dryden's method here is something very near to parody; he applies vocabulary, images, and ceremony which arouse epic associations of grandeur, to make an enemy helplessly ridiculous. But the effect, though disastrous for the enemy, is very different from that of the humour which merely belittles, such as the satire of Mark Twain. Dryden continually enhances: he makes his object great, in a way contrary to expectation; and the total effect is due to the transformation of the ridiculous into poetry. As an example may be taken a fine passage plagiarized from Cowley, from lines which Dryden must have marked well, for he quotes them directly in one of his prefaces. Here is Cowley:—

> Where their vast courts the mother-waters keep,
> And undisturbed by moons in silence sleep. . . .
> Beneath the dens where unfledged tempests lie,
> And infant winds their tender voices try.

In "MacFlecknoe" this becomes:—

> Where their vast courts the mother-strumpets keep,
> And undisturbed by watch, in silence sleep.
> Near these, a nursery erects its head,
> Where queens are formed, and future heroes bred;
> Where unfledged actors learn to laugh and cry,
> Where infant punks their tender voices try,
> And little Maximins the gods defy.

The passage from Cowley is by no means despicable verse. But it is a commonplace description of commonly poetic objects; it has not the element of *surprise* so essential to poetry, and this Dryden provides. A clever versifier might have written Cowley's lines; only a poet could have made what Dryden made of them. It is impossible to dismiss his verses as "prosaic"; turn them into prose and they are transmuted, the fragrance is gone. The reproach of the prosaic, levelled at Dryden, rests upon a confusion between the emotions considered to be poetic, which is a matter allowing considerable latitude of fashion, and the result of personal emotion in poetry; and, in the third place, there is the emotion depicted by the poet in some kinds of poetry, of which the "Testaments" of Villon is an example. Again, there is the intellect, the originality and independence and clarity of what we vaguely call the poet's "point of view." Our valuation of poetry, in short, depends upon several considerations, upon the permanent and upon the mutable and upon the transitory. When we try to isolate the essentially poetic, we bring our pursuit in the end to something insignificant; our standards vary with every poet whom we consider. All we can hope to do, in the attempt to introduce some order into our preferences, is to clarify our reasons for finding pleasure in the poetry that we like.

With regard to Dryden, therefore, we can say this much. Our taste in English poetry has been largely founded upon a partial perception of the value of Shakespeare and Milton, a perception which dwells upon sublimity of theme and action. Shakespeare had a great deal more; he had nearly everything to satisfy our various desires for poetry. The point is that the depreciation or neglect of Dryden is not due to the fact that his work is not poetry, but to a prejudice that the material, the feelings, out of which he built it is not poetic. Thus Matthew Arnold observes, in mentioning Dryden and Pope together, that "their poetry is conceived and composed in their wits, genuine poetry is conceived in the soul." Arnold was, perhaps, not altogether the detached critic when he wrote this line; he may have been stirred to a defence of his own poetry, conceived and composed in the soul of a mid-century Oxford graduate. Pater remarks that Dryden—

> Loved to emphasize the distinction between poetry and prose, the protest against their confusion coming with somewhat diminished effect from one whose poetry was so prosaic.

But Dryden was right, and the sentence of Pater is cheap journalism. Hazlitt, who had perhaps the most uninteresting mind of all our distinguished critics, says:—

> Dryden and Pope are the great masters of the artificial style of poetry in our language, as the poets of whom I have already treated— Chaucer, Spenser, Shakespeare, and Milton—were of the natural.

In one sentence Hazlitt has committed at least four crimes against taste. It is bad enough to lump Chaucer, Spenser, Shakespeare, and Milton together under the denomination of "natural"; it is bad to commit Shakespeare to one style only; it is bad to join Dryden and Pope together; but the last absurdity is the contrast of Milton, our greatest master of the *artificial* style, with Dryden, whose *style* (vocabulary, syntax, and order of thought) is in a high degree natural. And what all these objections come to, we repeat, is a repugnance for the material out of which Dryden's poetry is built.

It would be truer to say, indeed, even in the form of the unpersuasive paradox, that Dryden is distinguished principally by his *poetic* ability. We prize him, as we do Mallarmé, for what he made of his material. Our estimate is only in part the appreciation of ingenuity: in the end the result *is* poetry. Much of Dryden's unique merit consists in his ability to make the small into the great, the prosaic into the poetic, the trivial into the magnificent. In this he differs not only from Milton, who required a canvas of the largest size, but from Pope, who required one of the small-est. If you compare any satiric "character" of Pope with one of Dryden, you will see that the method and intention are widely divergent. When Pope alters, he diminishes; he is a master of miniature. The singular skill of his portrait of Addison, for example, in the "Epistle to Arbuthnot," depends upon the justice and reserve, the apparent determination not to exaggerate. The genius of Pope is not for caricature. But the effect of the portraits of Dryden is to transform the object into something greater, as were transformed the verses of Cowley quoted above.

> A fiery soul, which working out its way,
>      Fretted the pigmy body to decay:
>      And o'er informed the tenement of clay.

These lines are not merely a magnificent tribute. They create the object which they contemplate; the poetry is purer than anything in Pope except the last lines of the "Dunciad." Dryden is in fact much nearer to the mas-ter of comic creation than to Pope. As in Jonson, the effect is far from laughter; the comic is the material, the result is poetry. The Civic Guards of Rhodes—

> The country rings around with loud alarms,
> And raw in fields the rude militia swarms;
> Mouths without hands; maintained at vast expense,
> In peace a charge, in war a weak defence;

> Stout once a month they march, a blust'ring band,
> And ever, but in times of need, at hand;
> This was the morn, when issuing on the guard,
> Drawn up in rank and file they stood prepared
> Of seeming arms to make a short essay,
> Then hasten to be drunk, the business of the day.

Sometimes the wit appears as a delicate flavour to the magnificence, as in "Alexander's Feast":—

> Sooth'd with the sound the king grew vain;
> Fought all his battles o'er again;
> And thrice he routed all his foes, and thrice he
> slew the slain.

The great advantage of Dryden over Milton is that while the former is always in control of his ascent, and can rise or fall at will (and how masterfully, like his own Timotheus, he directs the transitions!), the latter has elected a perch from which he cannot afford to fall, and from which he is in danger of slipping.

> food alike those pure
> Intelligential substances require
> As doth your Rational; and both contain
> Within them every lower faculty
> Of sense, whereby they hear, see, smell, touch, taste,
> Tasting concoct, digest, assimilate,
> And corporeal to incorporeal turn.

Dryden might have made poetry out of that; his translation from Lucretius is poetry. But we have an ingenious example, on which to test our contrast of Dryden and Milton: it is Dryden's "Opera," called *The State of Innocence and Fall of Man*, of which Nathaniel Lee neatly says in his preface:—

> For Milton did the wealthy mine disclose,
> And rudely cast what you could well dispose:
> He roughly drew, on an old-fashioned ground,
> A chaos, for no perfect world were found,
> Till through the heap, your mighty genius shined.

In the author's preface Dryden acknowledges his debt generously enough:—

The original being undoubtedly, one of the greatest, most noble, and most sublime poems, which either this age or nation has produced.

The poem begins auspiciously:—

> *Lucifer:*  Is this the seat our conqueror has given?
> And this the climate we must change for Heaven?
> These regions and this realm my wars have got;
> This mournful empire is the loser's lot:
> In liquid burnings, or on dry to dwell,
> Is all the sad variety of hell.

It is an early work; it is on the whole a feeble work; it is not deserving of sustained comparison with "Paradise Lost." But "all the sad variety of Hell"! Dryden is already stirring; he has assimilated what he could from Milton; and he has shown himself capable of producing as splendid verse.

The capacity for assimilation, and the consequent extent of range, are conspicuous qualities of Dryden. He advanced and exhibited his variety by constant translation; and his translations of Horace, of Ovid, of Lucretius, are admirable. His gravest defects are supposed to be displayed in his dramas, but if these were more read they might be more praised. From the point of view of either the Elizabethan or the French drama they are obviously inferior; but the charge of inferiority loses part of its force if we admit that Dryden was not quite trying to compete with either, but was pursuing a direction of his own. He created no character; and although his arrangements of plot manifest exceptional ingenuity, it is the pure magnificence of diction, of poetic diction, that keeps his plays alive:—

> How I loved
> Witness ye days and nights, and all ye hours,
> That danced away with down upon your feet,
> As all your business were to count my passion.
> One day passed by, and nothing saw but love;
> Another came, and still 'twas only love:
> The suns were wearied out with looking on,
> And I untired with loving.
> I saw you every day and all the day;
> And every day was still but as the first:
> So eager was I still to see you more . . .
>
> While within your arms I lay,
> The world fell mould'ring from my hands each hour.

Such language is pure Dryden: it sounds, in Mr. van Doren's phrase, "like a gong." *All for Love,* from which the lines are taken, is Dryden's best play, and this is perhaps the highest reach. In general, he is best in his plays when dealing with situations which do not demand great emotional concentration; when his situation is more trivial, and he can practise his art of making the small great. The back-talk between the Emperor and his Empress Nourmahal, in *Aurungzebe,* is admirable purple comedy:—

> *Emperor.* Such virtue is the plague of human life:
> A virtuous woman, but a cursèd wife.
> In vain of pompous chastity y' are proud:
> Virtue's adultery of the tongue, when loud.
> I, with less pain, a prostitute could bear,
> Then the shrill sound of virtue, virtue hear.
> In unchaste wives—
> There's yet a kind of recompensing ease:
> Vice keeps 'em humble, gives 'em care to please:
> But against clamourous virtue, what defence?
> It stops our mouths, and gives your noise pretence. . . .
>
> What can be sweeter than our native home?
> Thither for ease, and soft repose, we come;
> Home is the sacred refuge of our life:
> Secure from all approaches but a wife.
> If thence we fly, the cause admits no doubt:
> None but an inmate foe could force us out.
> Clamours, our privacies uneasy make.
> Birds leave their nests disturbed, and
>    beasts their haunts forsake.

But drama is a mixed form; pure magnificence will not carry it through. The poet who attempts to achieve a play by the single force of the word provokes comparison, however strictly he confine himself to his capacity, with poets of other gifts. Corneille and Racine do not attain their triumphs by magnificence of this sort; they have concentration also, and, in the midst of their phrases, an undisturbed attention to the human soul as they knew it.

Nor is Dryden unchallenged in his supreme ability to make the ridiculous, or the trivial, great.

> Avez-vous observé que maints cercueils de vielles
> Sont presque aussi petits que celui d'un enfant?

Those lines are the work of a man whose verse is as magnificent as

Dryden's, and who could see profounder possibilities in wit, and in
Dryden's mind. For Dryden, with all his intellect, had a commonplace
mind. His powers were, we believe, wider, but no greater, than Milton's;
he was confined by boundaries as impassable, though less strait. He bears
a curious antithetical resemblance to Swinburne. Swinburne was also a
master of words, but Swinburne's words are all suggestions and no deto-
nation; if they suggest nothing, it is because they suggest too much.
Dryden's words, on the other hand, are precise, they state immensely, but
their suggestiveness is almost nothing.

> That short dark passage to a future state;
> That melancholy riddle of a breath.
> That something, or that nothing, after death,

is a riddle, but not melancholy enough, in Dryden's splendid verse. The
question, which has certainly been waiting, may justly be asked: whether
without this which Dryden lacks, poetry can exist? What is man to decide
what poetry is? Dryden's use of language is not, like that of Swinburne,
weakening and demoralizing. Let us take as a final test his elegy upon
Oldham, which deserves not to be mutilated:—

> Farewell, too little and too lately known,
> Whom I began to think and call my own;
> For sure our souls were near allied, and thine
> Cast in the same poetic mould with mine.
> One common note on either lyre did strike,
> And knaves and fools we both abhorred alike.
> To the same goal did both our studies drive;
> The last set out the soonest did arrive.
> Thus Nisus fell upon the slippery place,
> Whilst his young friend performed and won the race.
> O early ripe! to thy abundant store
> What could advancing age have added more?
> It might (what nature never gives the young)
> Have taught the numbers of thy native tongue.
> But satire needs not those, and wit will shine
> Through the harsh cadence of a rugged line.
> A noble error, and but seldom made,
> When poets are by too much force betrayed.
> Thy generous fruits, though gathered ere their prime,
> Still showed a quickness; and maturing time
> But mellows what we write to the dull sweets of rhyme.
> Once more, hail, and farewell; farewell, thou young,

But ah! too short, Marcellus of our tongue!
Thy brows with ivy and with laurels bound;
But fate and gloomy night encompass thee around.

From the perfection of such an elegy we cannot detract; the lack of nebula is compensated by the satisfying completeness of the statement.
Dryden lacked what his master Jonson possessed, a large and unique view
of life; he lacked insight, he lacked profundity. But where Dryden fails to
satisfy, the nineteenth century does not satisfy us either; and where that
century has condemned him, it is itself condemned. In the next revolution of taste it is possible that poets may turn to the study of Dryden. He
remains one of those who have set standards for English verse which it is
desperate to ignore.

# THE METAPHYSICAL POETS

B Y collecting these poems[1] from the work of a generation more often named than read, and more often read than profitably studied, Professor Grierson has rendered a service of some importance. Certainly the reader will meet with many poems already preserved in other anthologies, at the same time that he discovers poems such as those of Aurelian Townshend or Lord Herbert of Cherbury here included. But the function of such an anthology as this is neither that of Professor Saintsbury's admirable edition of Caroline poets nor that of the "Oxford Book of English Verse." Mr. Grierson's book is in itself a piece of criticism, and a provocation of criticism; and we think that he was right in including so many poems of Donne, elsewhere (though not in many editions) accessible, as documents in the case of "metaphysical poetry." The phrase has long done duty as a term of abuse, or as the label of a quaint and pleasant taste. The question is to what extent the so-called metaphysicals formed a school (in our own time we should say a "movement"), and how far this so-called school or movement is a digression from the main current.

Not only is it extremely difficult to define metaphysical poetry, but difficult to decide what poets practise it and in which of their verses. The poetry of Donne (to whom Marvell and Bishop King are sometimes nearer than any of the other authors) is late Elizabethan, its feeling often very close to that of Chapman. The "courtly" poetry is derivative from Jonson, who borrowed liberally from the Latin; it expires in the next century with the sentiment and witticism of Prior. There is finally the devotional verse of Herbert, Vaughan and Crashaw (echoed long after by Christina Rossetti and Francis Thompson); Crashaw, sometimes more profound and less sectarian than the others, has a quality which returns through the Elizabethan period to the early Italians. It is difficult to find any precise

---

[1] *Metaphysical Lyrics and Poems of the Seventeenth Century: Donne to Butler.* Selected and edited, with an Essay, by Herbert J. C. Grierson (Oxford: Clarendon Press. London: Milford).

use of metaphor, simile, or other conceit, which is common to all the poets and at the same time important enough as an element of style to isolate these poets as a group. Donne, and often Cowley, employ a device which is sometimes considered characteristically "metaphysical": the elaboration (contrasted with the condensation) of a figure of speech to the farthest stage to which ingenuity can carry it. Thus Cowley develops the commonplace comparison of the world to a chess-board through long stanzas ("To Destiny"), and Donne, with more grace, in "A Valediction," the comparison of two lovers to a pair of compasses. But elsewhere we find, instead of the mere explication of the content of a comparison, a development by rapid association of thought which requires considerable agility on the part of the reader.

> On a round ball
> A workeman that hath copies by, can lay
> An Europe, Afrique, and an Asia.
> And quickly make that, which was nothing, *All,*
> So doth each teare,
> Which thee doth weare,
> A globe, yea world by that impression grow,
> Till thy tears mixt with mine doe overflow
> This world, by waters sent from thee, my heaven
> dissolved so.

Here we find at least two connexions which are not implicit in the first figure, but are forced upon it by the poet: from the geographer's globe to the tear, and the tear to the deluge. On the other hand, some of Donne's most successful and characteristic effects are secured by brief words and sudden contrasts:—

> A bracelet of bright hair about the bone,

where the most powerful effect is produced by the sudden contrast of associations of "bright hair" and of "bone." This telescoping of images and multiplied association is characteristic of the phrase of some of the dramatists of the period which Donne knew: not to mention Shakespeare, it is frequent in Middleton, Webster and Tourneur, and is one of the sources of the vitality of their language.

Johnson, who employed the term "metaphysical poets," apparently having Donne, Cleveland and Cowley chiefly in mind, remarks of them that "the most heterogenous ideas are yoked by violence together." The force of this impeachment lies in the failure of the conjunction, the fact that often the ideas are yoked but not united; and if we are to judge of styles of poetry by their abuse, enough examples may be found in Cleveland to justify Johnson's condemnation. But a degree of heterogeneity of material compelled into unity by the operation of the poet's mind is omnipresent in poetry. We need not select for illustration such a line as:—

> Notre âme est un trois-mâts cherchant son Icarie;

we may find it in some of the best lines of Johnson himself ("The Vanity of Human Wishes"):—

> His fate was destined to a barren strand,
> A petty fortress, and a dubious hand;
> He left a name at which the world grew pale,
> To point a moral, or adorn a tale,

where the effect is due to a contrast of ideas, different in degree but the same principle, as that which Johnson mildly reprehended. And in one of the finest poems of the age (a poem which could not have been written in any other age), the "Exequy" of Bishop King, the extended comparison is used with perfect success: the idea and the simile become one, in the passage in which the Bishop illustrates his impatience to see his dead wife, under the figure of a journey:—

> Stay for me there; I will not faile
> To meet thee in that hollow Vale.
> And think not much of my delay;
> I am already on the way,
> And follow thee with all the speed
> Desire can make, or sorrows breed.
> Each minute is a short degree.
> And ev'ry houre a step towards thee.
> At night when I betake to rest,
> Next morn I rise nearer my West
> Of life, almost by eight houres sail,
> Than when sleep breath'd his drowsy gale. . . .
> But heark! My Pulse, like a soft Drum
> Beats my approach, tells *Thee* I come;
> And slow howere my marches be,
> I shall at last sit down by *Thee*.

(In the last few lines there is that effect of terror which is several times attained by one of Bishop King's admirers, Edgar Poe). Again, we may justly take these quatrains from Lord Herbert's Ode, stanzas which would, we think, be immediately pronounced to be of the metaphysical school:—

> So when from hence we shall be gone,
>   And be no more, nor you, nor I,
>   As one another's mystery,
> Each shall be both, yet both but one.
>
> This said, in her up-lifted face,
>   Her eyes, which did that beauty crown,
>   Were like two starrs, that having faln down,
> Look up again to find their place:
>
> While such a moveless silent peace
>   Did seize on their becalmed sense,
>   One would have thought some influence
> Their ravished spirits did possess.

There is nothing in these lines (with the possible exception of the stars, a simile not at once grasped, but lovely and justified) which fits Johnson's general observations on the metaphysical poets in his essay on Cowley. A good deal resides in the richness of association which is at the same time borrowed from and given to the word "becalmed"; but the meaning is clear, the language simple and elegant. It is to be observed that the language of these poets is as a rule simple and pure; in the verse of George Herbert this simplicity is carried as far as it can go—a simplicity emulated without success by numerous modern poets. The *structure* of the sentences, on the other hand, is sometimes far from simple, but this is not a vice: it is a fidelity to thought and feeling. The effect, at its best, is far less artificial than that of an ode by Gray. And as this fidelity induces variety of thought and feeling, so it induces variety of music. We doubt whether, in the eighteenth century, could be found two poems in nominally the same metre, so dissimilar as Marvell's "Coy Mistress" and Crashaw's "Saint Teresa"; the one producing an effect of great speed by the use of short syllables, and the other an ecclesiastical solemnity by the use of long ones:—

> Love, thou art absolute sole lord
> Of life and death.

If so shrewd and sensitive (though so limited) a critic as Johnson failed to define metaphysical poetry by its faults, it is worth while to inquire whether we may not have more success by adopting the opposite method: by assuming that the poets of the seventeenth century (up to the Revolution) were the direct and normal development of the precedent age; and, without prejudicing their case by the adjective "metaphysical," consider whether their virtue was not something permanently valuable, which subsequently disappeared, but ought not to have disappeared. Johnson has hit, perhaps by accident, on one of their peculiarities when he observes that "their attempts were always analytic"; he would not agree that, after the dissociation, they put the material together again in a new unity.

It is certain that the dramatic verse of the later Elizabethan and early Jacobean poets expresses a degree of development of sensibility which is not found in any of the prose, good as it often is. If we except Marlowe, a man of prodigious intelligence, these dramatists were directly or indirectly (it is at least a tenable theory) affected by Montaigne. Even if we except also Jonson and Chapman, these two were notably erudite, and were notably men who incorporated their erudition into their sensibility: their mode of feeling was directly and freshly altered by their reading and thought. In Chapman especially there is a direct sensuous apprehension of thought into feeling, which is exactly what we find in Donne:—

> in this one thing, all the discipline
> Of manners and of manhood is contained;
> A man to join himself with th' Universe
> In his main sway, and make in all things fit
> One with that All, and go on, round as it;
> Not plucking from the whole his wretched part,
> And into straits, or into nought revert,
> Wishing the complete Universe might be
> Subject to such a rag of it as he;
> But to consider great Necessity.

We compare this with some modern passage:—

> No, when the fight begins within himself,
> A man's worth something. God stoops o'er his head,
> Satan looks up between his feet—both tug—
> He's left, himself, i' the middle; the soul wakes
> And grows. Prolong that battle through his life!

It is perhaps somewhat less fair, though very tempting (as both poets are concerned with the perpetuation of love by offspring), to compare with the stanzas already quoted from Lord Herbert's Ode the following from Tennyson:—

> One walked between his wife and child,
> With measured footfall firm and mild,
> And now and then he gravely smiled.
>     The prudent partner of his blood
>     Leaned on him, faithful, gentle, good,
>     Wearing the rose of womanhood.
> And in their double love secure,
> The little maiden walked demure,
> Pacing with downward eyelids pure.
>     These three made unity so sweet,
>     My frozen heart began to beat,
>     Remembering its ancient heat.

The difference is not a simple difference of degree between poets. It is something which had happened to the mind of England between the time of Donne or Lord Herbert of Cherbury and the time of Tennyson and Browning; it is the difference between the intellectual poet and the reflective poet. Tennyson and Browning are poets, and they think; but they do not feel their thought as immediately as the odour of a rose. A thought to Donne was an experience; it modified his sensibility. When a poet's mind is perfectly equipped for its work, it is constantly amalgamating disparate experience; the ordinary man's experience is chaotic, irregular, fragmentary. The latter falls in love, or reads Spinoza, and these two experiences have nothing to do with each other, or with the noise of the typewriter or the smell of cooking; in the mind of the poet these experiences are always forming new wholes.

We may express the difference by the following theory: The poets of the seventeenth century, the successors of the dramatists of the sixteenth, possessed a mechanism of sensibility which could devour any kind of experience. They are simple, artificial, difficult, or fantastic, as their predecessors were; no less nor more than Dante, Guido Cavalcanti, Guinizelli, or Cino. In the seventeenth century a dissociation of sensibility set in, from which we have never recovered; and this dissociation, as is natural, was due to the influence of the two most powerful poets of the century, Milton and Dryden. Each of these men performed certain poetic functions so magnificently well that the magnitude of the effect concealed the absence of others. The language went on and in some respects improved; the best verse of Collins, Gray, Johnson, and even Goldsmith satisfies some of our fastidious demands better than that of Donne or Marvell or King. But while the language became more refined, the feeling became more crude. The feeling, the sensibility, expressed in the "Country Churchyard" (to say nothing of Tennyson and Browning) is cruder than that in the "Coy Mistress."

The second effect of the influence of Milton and Dryden followed from the first, and was therefore slow in manifestation. The sentimental age began early in the eighteenth century, and continued. The poets revolted against the ratiocinative, the descriptive; they thought and felt by fits, unbalanced; they reflected. In one or two passages of Shelley's "Triumph of Life," in the second "Hyperion," there are traces of a struggle toward unification of sensibility. But Keats and Shelley died, and Tennyson and Browning ruminated.

After this brief exposition of a theory—too brief, perhaps, to carry conviction—we may ask, what would have been the fate of the "metaphysical" had the current of poetry descended in a direct line from them, as it descended in a direct line to them? They would not, certainly, be classified as metaphysical. The possible interests of a poet are unlimited; the more intelligent he is the better; the more intelligent he is the more likely that he will have interests: our only condition is that he turn them into poetry, and not merely meditate on them poetically. A philosophical theory which has entered into poetry is established, for its truth or falsity in one sense ceases to matter, and its truth in another sense is proved. The poets in question have, like other poets, various faults. But they were, at best, engaged in the task of trying to find the verbal equivalent for states of mind and feeling. And this means both that they are more mature, and that they wear better, than later poets of certainly not less literary ability.

It is not a permanent necessity that poets should be interested in philosophy, or in any other subject. We can only say that it appears likely that poets in our civilization, as it exists at present, must be *difficult*. Our civilization comprehends great variety and complexity, and this variety and complexity, playing upon a refined sensibility, must produce various and complex results. The poet must become more and more comprehensive, more allusive, more indirect, in order to force, to dislocate if necessary, language into his meaning. (A brilliant and extreme statement of this view, with which it is not requisite to associate oneself, is that of M. Jean Epstein, "La Poésie d'aujourd'hui.") Hence we get something which looks very much like the conceit—we get, in fact, a method curiously similar to that of the "metaphysical poets," similar also in its use of obscure words and of simple phrasing.

O géraniums diaphanes, guerroyeurs sortilèges,
Sacrilèges monomanes!
Emballages, dévergondages, douches! O pressoirs
Des vendanges des grands soirs!
Layettes aux abois,
Thyrses au fond des bois!
Transfusions, représailles,
Relevailles, compresses et l'éternal potion,
Angélus! n'en pouvoir plus
De débâcles nuptiales! de débâcles nuptiales!

The same poet could write also simply:—

Elle est bien loin, elle pleure,
Le grand vent se lamente aussi . . .

Jules Laforgue, and Tristan Corbière in many of his poems, are nearer to
the "school of Donne" than any modern English poet. But poets more
classical than they have the same essential quality of transmuting ideas
into sensations, of transforming an observation into a state of mind.

Pour l'enfant, amoureux de cartes et d'estampes,
L'univers est égal à son vaste appétit.
Ah, que le monde est grand à la clarté des lampes!
Aux yeux du souvenir que le monde est petit!

In French literature the great master of the seventeenth century—
Racine—and the great master of the nineteenth—Baudelaire—are more
like each other than they are like anyone else. The greatest two masters
of diction are also the greatest two psychologists, the most curious explor-
ers of the soul. It is interesting to speculate whether it is not a misfortune
that two of the greatest masters of diction in our language, Milton and
Dryden, triumph with a dazzling disregard of the soul. If we continued to
produce Miltons and Drydens it might not so much matter, but as things
are it is a pity that English poetry has remained so incomplete. Those
who object to the "artificiality" of Milton or Dryden sometimes tell us to
"look into our hearts and write." But that is not looking deep enough;
Racine or Donne looked into a good deal more than the heart. One must
look into the cerebral cortex, the nervous system, and the digestive tracts.
    May we not conclude, then, that Donne, Crashaw, Vaughan, Herbert
and Lord Herbert, Marvell, King, Cowley at his best, are in the direct
current of English poetry, and that their faults should be reprimanded by

this standard rather than coddled by antiquarian affection? They have been enough praised in terms which are implicit limitations because they are "metaphysical" or "witty," "quaint" or "obscure," though at their best they have not these attributes more than other serious poets. On the other hand, we must not reject the criticism of Johnson (a dangerous person to disagree with) without having mastered it, without having assimilated the Johnsonian canons of taste. In reading the celebrated passage in his essay on Cowley we must remember that by wit he clearly means something more serious than we usually mean to-day; in his criticism of their versification we must remember in what a narrow discipline he was trained, but also how well trained; we must remember that Johnson tortures chiefly the chief offenders, Cowley and Cleveland. It would be a fruitful work, and one requiring a substantial book, to break up the classification of Johnson (for there has been none since) and exhibit these poets in all their difference of kind and of degree, from the massive music of Donne to the faint, pleasing tinkle of Aurelian Townshend—whose "Dialogue between a Pilgrim and Time" is one of the few regrettable omissions from this excellent anthology.

A CATALOG OF SELECTED

## DOVER BOOKS

IN ALL FIELDS OF INTEREST

# A CATALOG OF SELECTED DOVER
# BOOKS IN ALL FIELDS OF INTEREST

100 BEST-LOVED POEMS, Edited by Philip Smith. "The Passionate Shepherd to His Love," "Shall I compare thee to a summer's day?" "Death, be not proud," "The Raven," "The Road Not Taken," plus works by Blake, Wordsworth, Byron, Shelley, Keats, many others. 96pp. 5³⁄₁₆ x 8¼. 0-486-28553-7

100 SMALL HOUSES OF THE THIRTIES, Brown-Blodgett Company. Exterior photographs and floor plans for 100 charming structures. Illustrations of models accompanied by descriptions of interiors, color schemes, closet space, and other amenities. 200 illustrations. 112pp. 8⅜ x 11. 0-486-44131-8

1000 TURN-OF-THE-CENTURY HOUSES: With Illustrations and Floor Plans, Herbert C. Chivers. Reproduced from a rare edition, this showcase of homes ranges from cottages and bungalows to sprawling mansions. Each house is meticulously illustrated and accompanied by complete floor plans. 256pp. 9⅜ x 12¼.
0-486-45596-3

101 GREAT AMERICAN POEMS, Edited by The American Poetry & Literacy Project. Rich treasury of verse from the 19th and 20th centuries includes works by Edgar Allan Poe, Robert Frost, Walt Whitman, Langston Hughes, Emily Dickinson, T. S. Eliot, other notables. 96pp. 5³⁄₁₆ x 8¼. 0-486-40158-8

101 GREAT SAMURAI PRINTS, Utagawa Kuniyoshi. Kuniyoshi was a master of the warrior woodblock print — and these 18th-century illustrations represent the pinnacle of his craft. Full-color portraits of renowned Japanese samurais pulse with movement, passion, and remarkably fine detail. 112pp. 8⅜ x 11. 0-486-46523-3

ABC OF BALLET, Janet Grosser. Clearly worded, abundantly illustrated little guide defines basic ballet-related terms: arabesque, battement, pas de chat, relevé, sissonne, many others. Pronunciation guide included. Excellent primer. 48pp. 4³⁄₁₆ x 5¾.
0-486-40871-X

ACCESSORIES OF DRESS: An Illustrated Encyclopedia, Katherine Lester and Bess Viola Oerke. Illustrations of hats, veils, wigs, cravats, shawls, shoes, gloves, and other accessories enhance an engaging commentary that reveals the humor and charm of the many-sided story of accessorized apparel. 644 figures and 59 plates. 608pp. 6 ⅛ x 9¼.
0-486-43378-1

ADVENTURES OF HUCKLEBERRY FINN, Mark Twain. Join Huck and Jim as their boyhood adventures along the Mississippi River lead them into a world of excitement, danger, and self-discovery. Humorous narrative, lyrical descriptions of the Mississippi valley, and memorable characters. 224pp. 5³⁄₁₆ x 8¼. 0-486-28061-6

ALICE STARMORE'S BOOK OF FAIR ISLE KNITTING, Alice Starmore. A noted designer from the region of Scotland's Fair Isle explores the history and techniques of this distinctive, stranded-color knitting style and provides copious illustrated instructions for 14 original knitwear designs. 208pp. 8⅜ x 10⅞. 0-486-47218-3

Browse over 9,000 books at www.doverpublications.com

CATALOG OF DOVER BOOKS

ALICE'S ADVENTURES IN WONDERLAND, Lewis Carroll. Beloved classic about a little girl lost in a topsy-turvy land and her encounters with the White Rabbit, March Hare, Mad Hatter, Cheshire Cat, and other delightfully improbable characters. 42 illustrations by Sir John Tenniel. 96pp. 5³⁄₁₆ x 8¼.                        0-486-27543-4

AMERICA'S LIGHTHOUSES: An Illustrated History, Francis Ross Holland. Profusely illustrated fact-filled survey of American lighthouses since 1716. Over 200 stations — East, Gulf, and West coasts, Great Lakes, Hawaii, Alaska, Puerto Rico, the Virgin Islands, and the Mississippi and St. Lawrence Rivers. 240pp. 8 x 10¾.
0-486-25576-X

AN ENCYCLOPEDIA OF THE VIOLIN, Alberto Bachmann. Translated by Frederick H. Martens. Introduction by Eugene Ysaye. First published in 1925, this renowned reference remains unsurpassed as a source of essential information, from construction and evolution to repertoire and technique. Includes a glossary and 73 illustrations. 496pp. 6⅛ x 9¼.                        0-486-46618-3

ANIMALS: 1,419 Copyright-Free Illustrations of Mammals, Birds, Fish, Insects, etc., Selected by Jim Harter. Selected for its visual impact and ease of use, this outstanding collection of wood engravings presents over 1,000 species of animals in extremely lifelike poses. Includes mammals, birds, reptiles, amphibians, fish, insects, and other invertebrates. 284pp. 9 x 12.                        0-486-23766-4

THE ANNALS, Tacitus. Translated by Alfred John Church and William Jackson Brodribb. This vital chronicle of Imperial Rome, written by the era's great historian, spans A.D. 14-68 and paints incisive psychological portraits of major figures, from Tiberius to Nero. 416pp. 5³⁄₁₆ x 8¼.                        0-486-45236-0

ANTIGONE, Sophocles. Filled with passionate speeches and sensitive probing of moral and philosophical issues, this powerful and often-performed Greek drama reveals the grim fate that befalls the children of Oedipus. Footnotes. 64pp. 5³⁄₁₆ x 8 ¼.                        0-486-27804-2

ART DECO DECORATIVE PATTERNS IN FULL COLOR, Christian Stoll. Reprinted from a rare 1910 portfolio, 160 sensuous and exotic images depict a breathtaking array of florals, geometrics, and abstracts — all elegant in their stark simplicity. 64pp. 8⅜ x 11.                        0-486-44862-2

THE ARTHUR RACKHAM TREASURY: 86 Full-Color Illustrations, Arthur Rackham. Selected and Edited by Jeff A. Menges. A stunning treasury of 86 full-page plates span the famed English artist's career, from Rip Van Winkle (1905) to masterworks such as Undine, A Midsummer Night's Dream, and Wind in the Willows (1939). 96pp. 8⅜ x 11.
0-486-44685-9

THE AUTHENTIC GILBERT & SULLIVAN SONGBOOK, W. S. Gilbert and A. S. Sullivan. The most comprehensive collection available, this songbook includes selections from every one of Gilbert and Sullivan's light operas. Ninety-two numbers are presented uncut and unedited, and in their original keys. 410pp. 9 x 12.
0-486-23482-7

THE AWAKENING, Kate Chopin. First published in 1899, this controversial novel of a New Orleans wife's search for love outside a stifling marriage shocked readers. Today, it remains a first-rate narrative with superb characterization. New introductory Note. 128pp. 5³⁄₁₆ x 8¼.                        0-486-27786-0

BASIC DRAWING, Louis Priscilla. Beginning with perspective, this commonsense manual progresses to the figure in movement, light and shade, anatomy, drapery, composition, trees and landscape, and outdoor sketching. Black-and-white illustrations throughout. 128pp. 8⅜ x 11.                        0-486-45815-6

Browse over 9,000 books at www.doverpublications.com